# HERITAGE CRAFTS TODAY

# Theorem Painting

# Theorem Painting

## Tips, Tools, and Techniques for Learning the Craft

**LINDA E. BRUBAKER**

*Photography by Kevin Brett*

STACKPOLE
BOOKS

*To my students,*
*who have encouraged me and*
*been encouraged by me over the years*

Published by
STACKPOLE BOOKS
5067 Ritter Road
Mechanicsburg, PA 17055
www.stackpolebooks.com

## Warning

Making theorems requires the use of oil paints. It is recommended to the reader that all the painting is done in a well-ventilated area. Paints and paint supplies and their fumes may cause irritation to the eyes and skin. All persons following the steps for painting in this book do so at their own risk. The author and publisher disclaim any and all liability for any injuries that may result from the execution of the steps provided here.

Printed in China

10 9 8 7 6 5 4 3 2 1

FIRST EDITION

Cover design by Tracy Patterson

Frontispiece: Wreath of flowers, birds, and butterflies with compote of fruit in the center by Linda E. Brubaker, 2007.

**Library of Congress Cataloging-in-Publication Data**

Brubaker, Linda E.
    Theorem painting : tips, tools, and techniques for learning the craft / Linda E. Brubaker ; photography by Kevin Brett. — 1st ed.
      p.    cm. — (Heritage crafts today)
    Includes bibliographical references.
    ISBN-13: 978-0-8117-0475-5 (hardcover, spiral bound)
    ISBN-10: 0-8117-0475-0 (hardcover, spiral bound)
    1. Textile painting.  2. Stencil work.  3. Folk art—United States.  I. Title.

TT851.B796   2009
746.6—dc22

2009001260

# CONTENTS

*Acknowledgments* . . . . . . . . . . . . . . . . . . . . . . 6

*Introduction* . . . . . . . . . . . . . . . . . . . . . . . 7

A Brief History of Theorem Painting . . . . . . . 9

Tools and Materials . . . . . . . . . . . . . . . . . . . 15

Basic Skills . . . . . . . . . . . . . . . . . . . . . . . . . . 23

Basic Painting Exercises . . . . . . . . . . . . . . . . 61

Project 1. Strawberry Wreath . . . . . . . . . . . 93

Project 2. Bleeding Heart Trinket Box . . . . 101

Project 3. American Copper Butterfly . . . . 107

Project 4. Canton Bowl of Cherries
and Apricots . . . . . . . . . . . . . . . . . . . . . . . 113

Project 5. Mallard Duck . . . . . . . . . . . . . . . 119

Project 6. Vase of Flowers . . . . . . . . . . . . . 129

Project 7. Memorial Theorem . . . . . . . . . . . 141

Project 8. Basket of Fruit . . . . . . . . . . . . . . 151

Project 9. Blue Vase of Flowers . . . . . . . . . 165

Framing . . . . . . . . . . . . . . . . . . . . . . . . . . . 179

Gallery . . . . . . . . . . . . . . . . . . . . . . . . . . . . 183

*Supplies and Resources* . . . . . . . . . . . . . . . . 189

*Bibliography* . . . . . . . . . . . . . . . . . . . . . . . 191

# ACKNOWLEDGMENTS

Many friends and students suggested that I write a book on theorem painting, and I thank them for their encouragement. I also appreciate Kyle Weaver, for giving me the opportunity to write this book, and Kevin Brett, who was a delight to work with, for his wonderful photography.

A special thank-you goes to my friend and student Jean Bellis, for her skill and patience in helping me polish the manuscript. Thanks also to Carolyn Clough and Alma Deal, for proofreading the patterns, and to students and friends who gave input on the patterns: Joan Bradford, Inda Graybill, Olivia Hill, Ann Kline, Cheryl Marsden, Susan Naddeo, Alexandra Perrot, and Mary Sweger.

I am grateful to the Heritage Center of Lancaster County, Pennsylvania; the New York Historical Association, Cooperstown, New York; private collectors; and other painters, for lending me their works to be photographed for this publication.

Three special friends were such great cheerleaders on this project: Jeanette Biddle, Dottie Eshleman, and Ruth Ann Lyond. Many thanks, dear friends. My deepest gratitude goes to my husband, Jim, for all his encouragement, computer help, and love. And last, to my children, Steven and Laura, who grew up around my paints.

# INTRODUCTION

Theorem painting was a popular art form in the late eighteenth and early nineteenth centuries. Most often it was taught to young ladies in fashionable academies as a "branch of knowledge." This style of painting is done both freehand and with a set of stencils, and theorems were painted with either oil pigments or watercolors. Most antique theorems painted on paper and silk were executed with watercolors, but this book focuses on the style of theorems painted with oil pigments on cotton velvet. The velvet gives the subject matter a realistic appearance.

My love affair with theorems began at a two-day workshop more than thirty years ago. I was hooked, and theorems have been a major part of my life ever since.

*Summer Flowers by Linda E. Brubaker. "A" award theorem painting from a pattern (No. 122) belonging to the Historical Society of Early American Decoration.* PRIVATE COLLECTION OF JAMES AND LINDA BRUBAKER

*Linda Brubaker in her studio.*

Above: *Bellpull by Linda E. Brubaker. Adaptation of a bellpull from a pattern in the book* The Art of Theorem Painting *by Linda Carter Lefko and Barbara Knickerbocker.* COLLECTION OF JAMES AND LINDA BRUBAKER

Left: *Pineapple by Linda E. Brubaker. Original pineapple design inspired by a hospitality symbol from Colonial days.* COLLECTION OF RICHARD AND SANDRA SENFT

Theorem painting portrays the natural world realistically, but in vivid hues that remind me of the bright colors in a box of crayons, which opened up a whole new world to me as a child. Such hues allowed me to color something based solely on my imagination. Thus began a lifelong love for color and all the beauty and joy it brings into our lives. The subtle transition of color on a seashell, flower petal, leaf, or piece of fruit transfixes me. The beauty of a velvety rose petal or the hard surface of a seashell illustrate both the complexity of nature and variations of color. In a theorem, particularly on velvet, a rose becomes almost lifelike and a shell three-dimensional.

Over the last thirty years, I have exhibited, demonstrated, and taught at various museums. I currently teach at Fletcher Farms School of Arts and Crafts in Ludlow, Vermont, and my own studio in Lititz, Pennsylvania. I am a juried member of the Historical Society of Early American Decoration and have received their coveted "A" award for excellence in painting numerous times. My work has been selected twice to decorate the White House Christmas tree and featured on HGTV's show *Decorating the White House.* I've also been selected as one of the top 200 traditional craftsmen by *Early American Life* magazine and have been honored to be one of its jurors for the *Directory of Traditional American Crafts.*

My curiosity about the origin and history of theorem painting led me to libraries and museums for research. What I found inspired me to create many new designs of my own. In the pages of this book are some wonderful examples of historic theorems from two of my favorite museums, the Heritage Center of Lancaster County and the New York Historical Association. The designs I have created for this book are for all skill levels and reflect the peace and tranquility of a bygone era.

I recommend that you start at the beginning and work through the chapters in sequence, as each design builds on the previous one, from easy to advanced. Experiment with color and have fun. Each person's paintings will look different and reflect that individual's personality. Come journey with me into the lovely, serene world of theorem painting.

# A Brief History of Theorem Painting

*Horace by M. A. Parker, 1825. This painting of the ancient Roman philosopher Horace was taken from a print of a painting by Angelica Kaufman, London, 1792. The colors of this oil-on-velvet literary theorem have remained bright and beautiful.* NEW YORK HISTORICAL ASSOCIATION

After gaining independence from England, the American colonies embraced all aspects of life and art. The economy of the new republic was growing and prospering, and upper-middle-class Americans wanted more education for their children. Not only were young men being educated, but young ladies' academies were springing up all over as well. The established schools had to expand, and some had waiting lists. The lessons taught were grouped into "branches," which included reading, writing, grammar, arithmetic, geography, history, and plain needlework. For an extra fee per semester, a young lady could also pursue music, drawing, and fine needlework. Theorem painting was brought by educators from England in the 1790s and was enthusiastically embraced. Each girl was encouraged to create her own composition and translate it into a theorem. But it also was acceptable to copy a teacher's work or an available print or painting, such as a French still life.

Theorems were seldom dated, but some have been found in New England dating back to 1792. The popularity of theorem painting was short-lived, however, lasting until the 1850s.

Although stencils were used, considerable skill was required to execute theorems properly. The process by which the early theorem painters created their stencil material was time-consuming. They prepared the paper with linseed oil, dried it, and then coated it several times with spirits of turpentine to make it stiff and waterproof. After the paper had dried, the parts of the drawing were numbered and the stencils traced and cut. To prepare the paints, pigments had to be ground with a mortar and pestle and mixed with linseed oil. The theorem paintings were then painted according to precise directions.

Landscapes, portraits, and memorial, literary, and religious scenes all were popular. But the most common subjects were floral bouquets, baskets of flowers and fruits, fruit compositions, birds, and butterflies. Flowers and fruits were favorites of the young ladies because they could be so realistically rendered. The bowls and baskets overflowed with fruit, sometimes seeming to defy gravity. A number of fine examples of baskets of fruit or fruit compositions are set on a mound of grass, tabletop, or a piece of marble.

Young ladies were taught grace and elegance in all their handiwork. They were expected to be proficient artists so that they could decorate their homes. A young

*Blue Vase of Flowers by Sarah Wilson, circa 1800. Sometimes a theorem can be dated by the basket or glass containers in the painting. For example, glass compotes were not produced until the 1830s.* COLLECTION OF JAMES AND LINDA BRUBAKER

*Oval Wreath of Flowers with Brown Bird and Cherries, by unknown artist. This beautiful unframed oval floral is a fine example of a carefully drawn floral design that was then worked into a theorem on velvet.* HERITAGE CENTER OF LANCASTER COUNTY, GIFT OF MRS. SARAH ELLMAKER MCILVANIE MUENCH

*Pitcher of Flowers with a Basket of Fruit, attributed to Wealthy O. Sawin, circa 1822. The drapery frames the still life of fruit and flowers. Sawin showed off her painting skill in the transition from one color to another on the fruit and flowers.* NEW YORK HISTORICAL ASSOCIATION

*Basket of Flowers by unknown artist. The pink cabbage roses in this flower basket hang their heads with the weight of many petals. Some of the red flowers have turned brown, but the red rose still has its fresh bloom.*

*Fruit in a White Bowl, attributed to Margaret Ann Freligh Platt, circa 1830–50. The artist was a teacher at the Plattsburg Academy. She received an education in both painting and teaching at Emma Willard's first school in Middlebury, Vermont. The colors of this oil-on-velvet theorem are still vibrant, but the reds have faded. The pineapple appears to have had a curve placed on the cutout and shaded from left to right, first with burnt sienna, and then moving to green.*

woman painted theorems not only to hang on her walls, but also for decorative pillows, embellishments on chairs, bellpulls, drawstring bags called reticules, watch pockets, and trinket boxes. After she married, she continued to pursue this art and decorated her home with theorems.

When painting theorems on such accoutrements, a certain deftness and surety were required. The deliberate graceful movement of the theorem painter's hands was a result of the strict teaching and the necessity of keeping paints and brushes neat. Moreover, a more difficult dimension was added by using watercolors instead of oils on velvet. The more artistic students might also translate their skill with oil paints to painting with watercolors on paper or silk.

Magazines such as *Godey's Lady's Book* included articles on velvet painting as early as 1830. Men, too, pursued theorem painting as a hobby. The Abby Aldrich Museum in Williamsburg, Virginia, has a wonderful piece painted by William Stearns around 1825, called *Still Life with Watermelon*. But as with all things that rapidly rise to be fashionable, eventually theorem painting

*Fruit on a Marble Slab by unknown artist. Many white spaces can be seen between the pieces of fruit in this oil-on-velvet theorem, but the artist skillfully created realistic-looking Thompson grapes and leaves. The tendrils were stenciled rather than freehand painted.* HERITAGE CENTER OF LANCASTER COUNTY, GIFT OF MRS. S. R. SLAYMAKER II

*Three Cups by Collata Holcomb, circa 1820–30. Elegance is simplicity in this beautifully rendered painting. The cups are mottled, giving the appearance of opaque glass containers, and the flowers spill out of them in graceful arcs.* NEW YORK HISTORICAL ASSOCIATION

began to wane, and in its place, Berlin needlework began to rise in popularity.

A renewed interest in theorem painting occurred in the years leading up to the American bicentennial, when there was a keen interest in reproducing items that were fashionable in the eighteenth and nineteenth centuries. People were researching and practicing the arts and crafts of our ancestors. Starting in the 1970s, homeowners wanted to decorate their homes with graceful reproduction velvet paintings. Some people like distressed, aged paintings, and that can be accomplished by dyeing the velvet in tea. Today the old-style theorems, with their peaceful, genteel beauty, are again being reproduced with skill and devotion by contemporary artists.

*Early Summer Bouquet by unknown artist, dated September 10, 1845. Watercolor theorems like this one were referred to as Oriental tinting or poonah work. These paintings on hard-surface paper lent themselves well to finer detail.*

HERITAGE CENTER OF LANCASTER COUNTY, GIFT OF MRS. SARAH ELLMAKER MCILVANIE MUENCH

*Floral Bouquet by unknown artist. Abundant linework was added to each of the flowers in this bouquet in oils on velvet.*

HERITAGE CENTER OF LANCASTER COUNTY, GIFT OF MRS. SARAH ELLMAKER MCILVANIE MUENCH

*Flowers of Love by unknown artist, circa 1830. When painting watercolors on silk, the artist had to know how to load her brush in such a manner that with one sure stroke, the color could be laid precisely and surely, keeping the paint from drying out or running under the stencil.*

COLLECTION OF JAMES AND LINDA BRUBAKER

*Memorial to Mrs. Gage by Miss Martha Gage. This memorial piece is a velvet theorem on which gold leaf foil was applied. The weathervane, bell, and doorknob of the church are gold leaf foil, as is the front door panel of the house, the lady's bangle bracelets, and the beads in the necklace and shoes of the little girl. Even the little dog has a collar of gold!*
NEW YORK HISTORICAL ASSOCIATION

*Portrait of a Young Girl by unknown artist, circa 1840. This portrait was painted with watercolors on paper. The artist used a stippling technique to paint the majority of this piece: the dress, drapery, flesh, landscaping, and flowers. The yellow flowers and the yellow petals on the pansies do not appear to have been stippled, however.* NEW YORK HISTORICAL ASSOCIATION

*Trinket Box by Susan Croasdale, 1834. Trinket boxes were embellished with theorem paintings. This painting of cascading flowers is encased with an embossed gold metallic paper. The cadmium red paint has faded and originally would have matched the paper on the box. The corners of this box have been reinforced with linen thread as was used on bandboxes.*
COLLECTION OF JAMES AND LINDA BRUBAKER

# Tools and Materials

For your work space, you need a flat surface on which to paint and a comfortable chair. You will also need a variety of tools and materials, as listed in this chapter. You can find many of the painting supplies at an art or craft store. Some items, such as the glass for cutting stencils, can be ordered from your local hardware store. For historic patterns, velvet, and other special items for theorem painting, see the Supplies section at the back of the book.

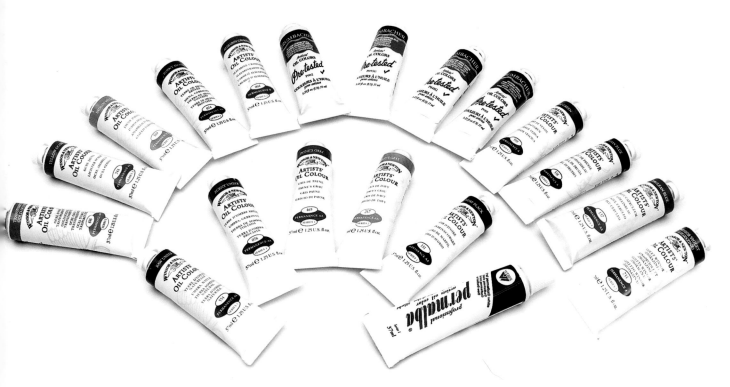

## PAINT

Use only artist-grade paints; student grades of paints will not give the same results as the colors shown in this book. It's also wise to use the recommended brands of paints as listed on the next page, because colors often vary from manufacturer to manufacturer. Burnt sienna, for example, is not the same hue in every brand. In this book, based on my thirty-plus years of painting, I have taken the guesswork out of deciding which paint brands to use.

The brands I recommend—Winsor and Newton, Grumbacher, and Weber—blend and mix beautifully and have proven over the years to give pleasing results time and again.

Here are the paints on velvet from the darkest to the lightest value to give you an idea of the colors.

**Winsor and Newton colors:**
- transparent gold ochre
- cadmium yellow light
- yellow ochre
- Indian yellow
- raw sienna
- burnt sienna
- alizarin crimson
- sap green
- Prussian blue
- cerulean blue
- Winsor violet
- burnt umber
- raw umber
- Payne's gray
- Davy's gray
- ivory black

**Grumbacher colors:**
- alizarin crimson golden
- Grumbacher red (a cadmium red)
- chromium oxide of green
- greenish umber

**Weber color:**
- Permalba white

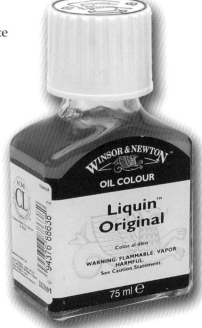

## LIQUIN

Liquin is a painting medium that is used occasionally on theorems, but only when you are instructed to do so in the directions. It is often mixed with oils when painting on a canvas, but usually no medium is necessary when painting on velvet. Where its use is specified on velvet, Liquin will make the paint a paler value of the color's natural hue.

When a theorem pattern calls for using Liquin and oil paints, follow these steps:

With your palette knife, pick up a little of the desired color from the top row of the palette and place it lower on the palette, below the color.

Remove some Liquin from the bottle and add to the paint on your palette. Mix well.

If the Liquin and paint are not well blended, the mixture will be streaky and cause problems when used for the painting.

When well blended, test your results on a scrap of velvet.

If the color needs to be adjusted, clean the palette knife and remove more Liquin from the bottle.

Place this Liquin below the mixed color, and then add some of the mixed color to the fresh Liquin.

Before picking up the adjusted color mixture with your brush, clean the first mixed color out of it by swirling it on a paper towel.

Pick up the newly adjusted color on your brush and test on the scrap of velvet.

## TURPENOID

A solvent manufactured by Weber Company, Turpenoid is an odorless synthetic turpentine. When mixed with oil paints, it allows them to flow smoothly and gives superior results when painting fine lines on velvet with a liner brush. With practice and the correct consistency of paint and Turpenoid, you can load a brush and dance across the velvet with a fine line for a long time. It also is a good cleaner for all your stencil brushes when you are finished painting.

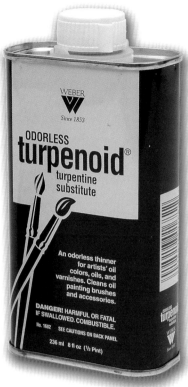

## BRUSHES

You need three styles of brushes for theorem painting. The ones you will reach for the most are the white round scrubbers by Scharff Brushes. Soft, natural-hair stencil brushes are also needed for subtle shading and some blending. For line and scroll work on velvet, the Scharff Series 480 Size 20/0 is a liner brush with great response.

## PAPER PALETTE PAD

This is used to place the pigments needed for your painting. A palette with a coating on each sheet works best. I use either a 9 x 12 or an 11 x 14-inch palette pad. This pad does not come with paint.

## MOUNTING BOARD

An excellent self-adhesive mounting board for theorem paintings on velvet is called Perfect Mount, made by Crescent Company. First cut the board to the exact size to fit in the rabbet drop of the frame (where the glass fits in the frame). Then peel off the back and place the sticky side down on the wrong side of the velvet. These boards measure 30 x 40 inches and can be purchased at a framing store.

## RULERS

Cork-backed rulers are a great aid for drawing your theorem paintings. When using one to draw a straight line, it will not slip and the line will stay true.

## CRAFT KNIVES

Purchase an X-acto knife and number 11 blades. The point on this blade is great for cutting stencils.

## STENCIL FILMS

For the purpose of photographing, I used a 3-mil plastic film. Trace on the dull side and cut on the shiny side. This plastic film can be purchased at any art store. Another good plastic film to use is Easy Cut Plastic, which is just as its name states.

## AVON SKIN SO SOFT OR BABY OIL

You will find many uses for this product. Add a drop or two of Avon Skin So Soft or baby oil to oil paint that has been thinned with Turpenoid. This helps keep the paint from wicking into the velvet too quickly. Dip your liner brush in Skin So Soft or baby oil after cleaning it in Turpenoid to help prevent the hairs from splitting and retain the pointed shape of the brush.

## PALETTE KNIVES

Palette knives come in many different styles and sizes. Purchase one with a bent handle, which will help keep your fingers from picking up paint while mixing colors. I prefer ones that are broader at the tip over those with a narrow, pointed tip.

## VELVET

You need 100 percent cotton velvet for painting theorems. It is sold by the yard and comes in widths of 44/45 inches or 52 inches from selvage to selvage. The velvet comes in soft white or ecru. It's a matter of personal preference which one to use. The ecru velvets give the theorems an older look and feel, whereas the white has a crisper appearance.

## TRACING PAPER

You will need both 9 x 12- and 11 x 14-inch tablets of tracing paper. When tracing your pattern onto the paper before painting, use an ink pen, as a pencil will smudge.

## GLASS

Use a ¼-inch-thick piece of glass approximately 13 x 17 inches for cutting stencils. Have the edges sanded and the corners rounded off to keep from cutting yourself. After tracing areas to be cut on stencil film, place the film on the glass and cut with an X-acto knife. Cut only the numbered sections indicated in directions.

## PERMANENT PEN AND WINDEX

The Micron .005 Permanent Pen works well on the different stencil films, although a regular pen is fine for those that have a very glossy surface. Use a little Windex to remove any ink that is left on the stencil film after the cutting is complete, so that it will not rub off onto the velvet. Place a paper towel under the cut stencil, and moisten another paper towel with Windex. Then gently wipe the ink off the edges of the stencil.

20

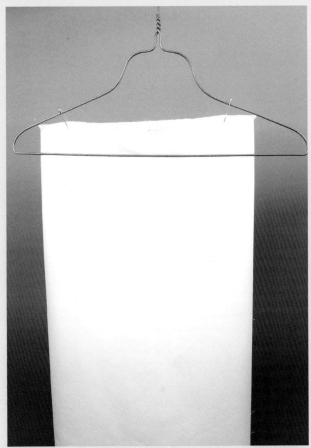

Sometimes the wrinkles are not completely removed with just the use of the steam iron. If not, wet a terry cloth or tea towel, and lay the damp cloth over the facedown velvet.

Hang velvet whenever possible. Smaller pieces can be stored by lying flat in a drawer or on a shelf. Do not store anything on top of the velvet; the nap will be crushed, and these deep impressions on the velvety surface cannot be removed. If the velvet is folded, it will develop creases or become wrinkled. You need to get any wrinkles out of the velvet before affixing it to the mounting board. The following instructions will enable you to eliminate most of the wrinkles.

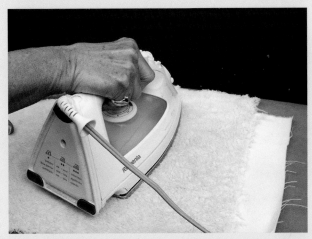

Then gently press the iron over the damp cloth. Remove the damp cloth and again press the velvet on the wrong side.

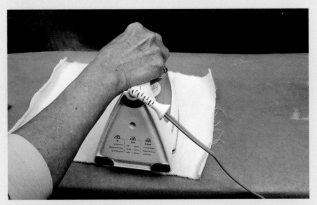

Lay the velvet facedown on the ironing board. With a steam iron set for cottons, press the wrong side of the velvet, carefully moving the iron over the surface.

Once the creases have been removed from the velvet, it is ready to be mounted on a mounting board.

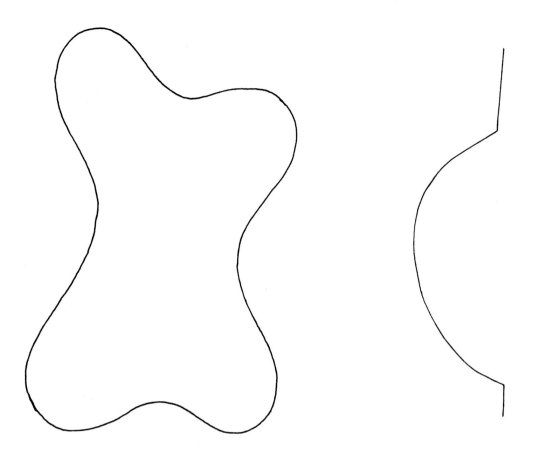

## SHIELDS

Cut several curved shields like the patterns provided, as well as several straight-edged shields about 1 x 4 inches. Cover areas not being painted with these shields to keep unwanted color off the surrounding openings on the stencil. The use of the shields also allows you to deepen the hue of an area without darkening surrounding areas.

## MURPHY'S OIL SOAP

Use this soap for removing any mistakes that occur on the painting. (See page 54.)

## WHITE GLUE

Any water-soluble pH-neutral glue will work for gluing the edges of the velvet to the back of the mounting board. You can find this type of glue in the scrapbooking section of any craft store.

# Basic Skills

Ｉn this chapter you will learn the skills
needed for making all theorem paintings.

- Preparing the mounting board
- Preparing the stencils
- Tea dyeing
- Mounting the velvet
- Straightening the grain of the velvet
- Mixing colors
- Painting a theorem
- Painting fine lines
- Removing painting mistakes
- Cleaning brushes

Cut a piece of board the exact size of the drawing. The example here will be a finished 9 x 12-inch board. I recommend using Crescent Perfect Mount.

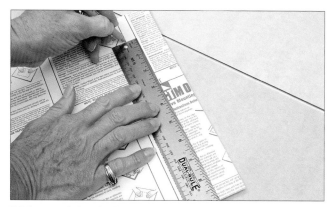

With a cork-backed ruler, mark three dots 9 inches from the edge for the length.

Line up the three dots with the ruler and draw a straight line. From the other edge of the mounting board, make three dots 12 inches in from the edge. Line up the ruler along the dots. Draw a straight line 12 inches long. You will have a 9 x 12-inch rectangle.

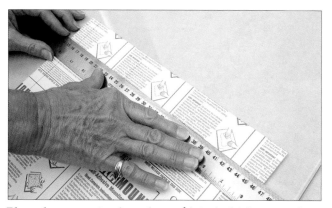

Place the mounting board on a 1/4-inch thick piece of glass. Then place the ruler along one line for guidance when cutting the mounting board.

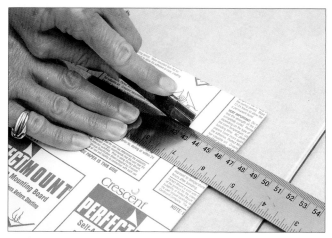

With an X-acto or utility knife, cut alongside the ruler. Move the ruler to the other line, and cut alongside the ruler and on the line. Sometimes the knife will not cut completely through the mounting board. Bend the scored mounting board.

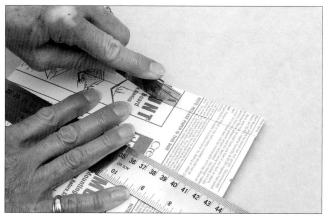

Carefully recut the mounting board along the scored line.

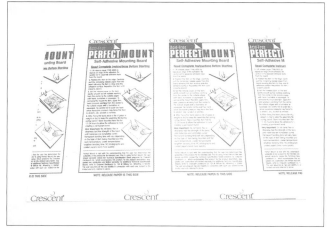

You now have a 9 x 12-inch piece of mounting board. Do not remove the adhesive backing at this time.

Many old theorems were framed tightly, without much space between the finished piece and the frame.

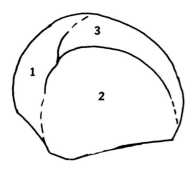

The Canton Bowl of Cherries and Apricots will serve as the example for stencil preparation. (This project can be found on page 113.) The following instructions will give your finished theorem a very pleasing appearance.

First determine the size of the theorem for painting. Then enlarge the design to the desired size. Add an extra 1 to 1 1/2 inches to each side of the drawing. This will determine the finished size of the painting. For example, if the actual design measures 5 x 7 inches, adding a total of 3 inches to both the width and length gives you an 8 x 10-inch finished painting.

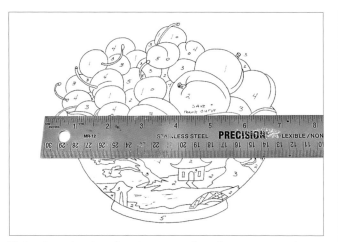

If the drawing is a fraction, round to the nearest inch for the framing size. For example, $5^3/4$ x $6^3/4$ inches—rounded up to 6 x 7—will still result in a finished size of 8 x 10. This added amount of space, $1^1/2$ inches all around, is an aesthetically balanced area that allows the theorem to fit comfortably in a frame without looking crowded. You will visually lose $1/4$ inch on each side of the painting's background because of the rabbet drop in space in the frame. This rabbet is the groove in the frame in which the picture rests. Most frames are sold by the drop-in measurement, such as 8 x 10, 9 x 12, or 16 x 20.

The next step is to prepare the stencil sheets. After determining the size of the finished painting, use a cork-backed ruler for marking and drawing lines for the stencil sheets.

Make three fairly equally spaced marks, measuring from the edge of the stencil film for the length needed. The Canton Bowl calls for an 8 x 10-inch frame, and you will need five 8 x 10-inch stencil sheets. Stencil film comes in varying widths. If the stencil film is 24 inches wide, make three marks 10 inches in from the edge the length of the stencil film.

Line up the three marks with the ruler and draw a straight line. Next, starting at one side of the 24-inch length, measure in 8 inches from the edge and make three marks along the length.

Draw another line along these three marks, and cut the sheets apart.

Now secure the drawing to a flat surface with masking tape.

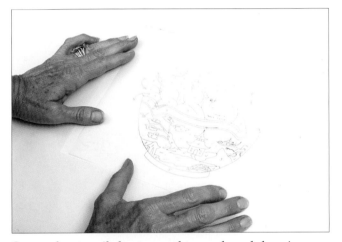

Center the stencil sheet over the numbered drawing, and then move the stencil ¼ inch lower than the center. This "weighting" gives the painting a much more pleasing look when framed. Secure the stencil sheet over the drawing with masking tape.

Draw a line along the corner edges of the stencil sheet to make registration marks for placement of subsequent sheets.

These registration marks will help keep the stencils in alignment.

Now you will trace the stencils. It is very important to be accurate when tracing a pattern, whether you are using tracing paper or the stencil film. If the stencil film has both a shiny and a matte side, trace on the matte side.

Use a fine-point pen; a Micron .005 works best. A point any wider than .01 will make the lines too thick, and you will wind up either over- or undercutting the stencils. If both sides of the stencil film are shiny, the Micron ink will rub off, so you need to start tracing at the top of the design to keep your hand off the ink. If this becomes a problem, switch to a regular ballpoint pen.

Take your time tracing. Use a separate stencil sheet for each number on the design.

Label each of the stencils in the upper left-hand corner with the title of the pattern, and under that, write the number of this stencil out of the total number required, such as #1 of 5. Mark any items on the stencil sheet "save" if indicated on the pattern.

Trace all the number 1 items onto the number 1 stencil sheet. Trace completely around each item on stencil 1.

**Stencil Number 1**

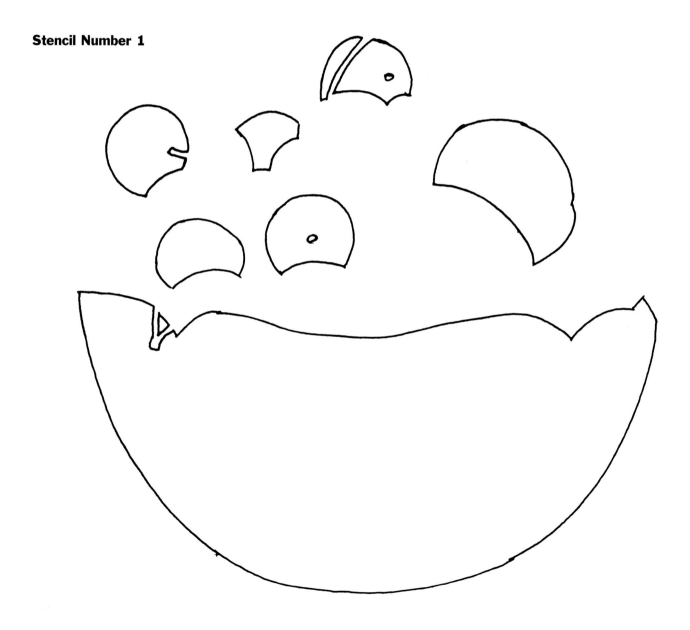

If you do not trace completely around the item, there will be a broken line when you remove the stencil from the drawing.

If you have missed tracing some lines, place the stencil sheet back into position and complete tracing the item. Trace the complete bowl, ignoring for now the decorations on the bowl, and mark it with "save."

Later, after the saved piece is cut out, you will tape it back in place. The overhanging cherry stem creates a triangle along the rim of the bowl on the left. Trace this triangle along with the large section of the bowl. This triangle will be cut into a tiny triangle and rectangles on two different stencils later, but treat it as one triangle for now. Remove the first completely traced stencil, and place a second sheet over the drawing within the registration marks you made earlier.

**Stencil Number 2**

Mark this stencil sheet #2 of 5. Trace only all the number 2 items to be cut out on this sheet. When finished, re-move this stencil sheet and position the third sheet on the drawing.

**Stencil Number 3**

Along the bowl rim on the left is a cherry that is split in two by a stem. Trace the small triangular part of the cherry on this third stencil sheet. Then trace all other items marked with the number 3. When that sheet is completed, move on to the next.

**Stencil Number 4**

On stencil 4, trace all items marked with a number 4.
Trace both sections of the cherries, which are divided by
stems. Trace the little triangle between the two apricots
along the bowl rim.

On stencil 5, trace all items marked with the number 5. Include the triangle on the band of the bowl between the cherry stem over the rim.

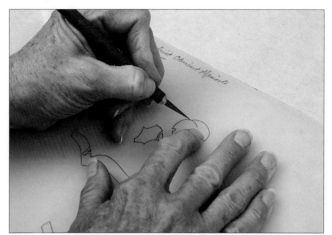

Now you will cut the stencils. Use a number 11 blade in your X-acto knife. Place the first traced stencil sheet on a piece of glass. Place the tip of the knife on one of the traced items. Press the knife into the stencil sheet, gently adding pressure until you hear a little pop. This sound indicates that you have cut completely through the stencil.

**Stencil Number 5**

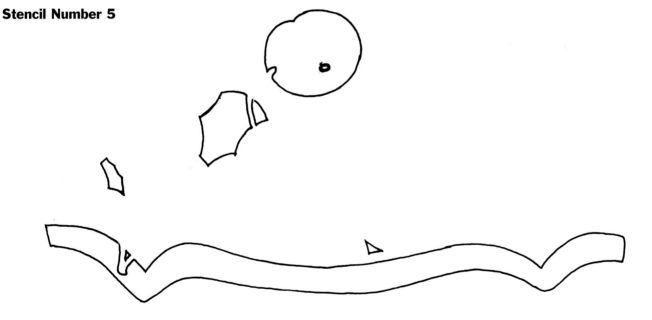

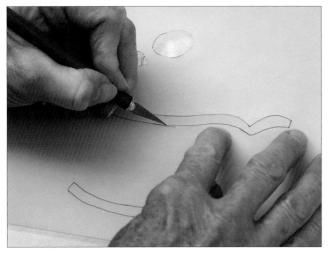

With one hand holding the stencil steady, pull the knife toward you along the traced line. You may rotate the stencil for a better cutting angle, but hold it firmly in one hand while cutting with the other. Cut the complete item out, following the lines carefully.

If the knife point gets dull or the tip has snapped off, change the blade. Put a piece of tape on the point before you dispose of it to avoid sticking yourself.

When cutting a curve or circle such as a grape, keep the X-acto knife stationary and turn the stencil with the other hand. You can turn the stencil as you cut in a very tight circle by walking the fingertips of one hand on the stencil, turning the stencil as you go while cutting with the other hand. When first starting to cut stencils, your cutting hand will get tired, and it is more difficult to cut stencils accurately with a tired hand. Take a break periodically and return later to cut some more.

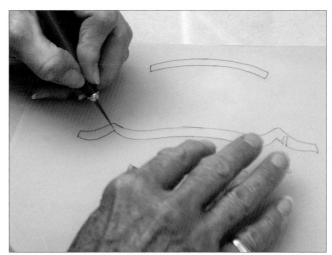

When cutting a long item, such as the rim on the bowl or a basket, hold the stencil sheet steady and pull the knife toward you.

Sometimes an item will be undercut. Try to avoid this. If you undercut an area, place your fingernail close to the line to be cut along the edge of an opening, and carefully trim off the area along the line.

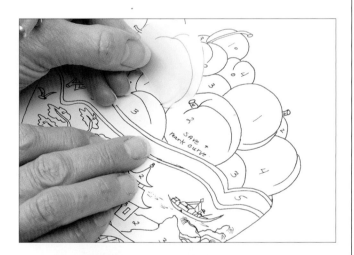

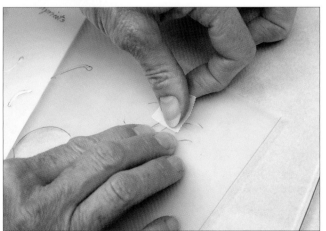

There are times when a pattern requires you to save a piece. On this pattern, the large apricot needs to be saved. Cut the apricot apart as required, and tape to the correct stencil.

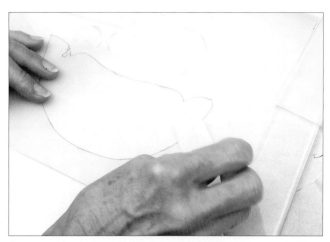

On stencil number 1, the large bowl is to be saved. Place the bowl piece in the stencil and tape it in place.

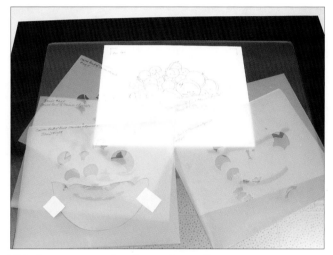

This is your completed set of stencils.

## Making Adjustments to an Uncentered Stencil

After a design has been traced, the stencils cut, and the painting completed and framed, you might find that it is not centered correctly. Here is how to fix the stencil so that it will be centered correctly for future paintings.

This apple painting is off-center, which will be very apparent when framed.

This apple painting is centered on the velvet board.

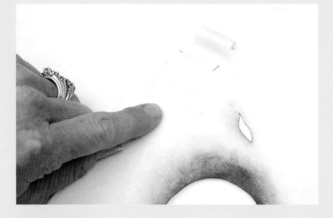

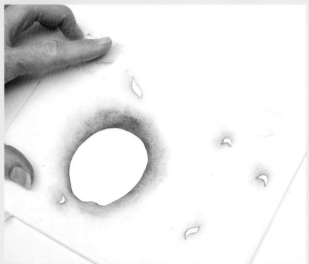

Before you use the stencils for this piece again, trim off either the top or bottom as needed to center the design. For this apple, the top of the stencil was trimmed and the notation marked on the stencil "place on top of velvet." This reminder will prevent future misplacement. To use, slide the stencil to the top, tape in place, put a shield along the bottom, and you can begin the painting.

Earlier in the book, there were examples of theorems that are 170 to 200 years old. Over time, these painting have suffered as a result of what we know today was improper framing or storage. Most of these framed pieces were sandwiched between glass and a backing made of wood. The wood leached acid, which damaged the velvet and paintings. Today we use acid-free mounting board and spacers when framing our artwork.

But some of us want to give our theorem paintings an old look. This can be achieved by dyeing the velvet in tea. Whether to dye your theorem before or after you have painted it is up to you. The paint colors will be muted if you dye the velvet afterward.

The following instructions are for dyeing the velvet by dipping it into the tea solution or using a sea sponge to apply the dye to the velvet.

*Tipped Bowl of Fruit by Linda E. Brubaker, 1986. The velvet on which this tipped bowl of fruit was painted was dyed before the painting was started.* COLLECTION OF STEVEN AND AMY BRUBAKER

## Supplies for Tea Dyeing

- black pekoe tea bags
- large bowl of hot water for tea infusion
- velvet
- sea sponge

Make a dye solution by placing hot water into a bowl along with three to five tea bags, depending on how dark you want to stain your velvet. Cool to room temperature. Remove the tea bags and squeeze lightly, taking care not to break the bags.

## DIP METHOD

Crumple the velvet into a ball in your hand. The tighter the ball, the more dramatic will be the staining.

Dip the crumpled ball of velvet in your hand into the tea infusion, and keep submerged for a few seconds.

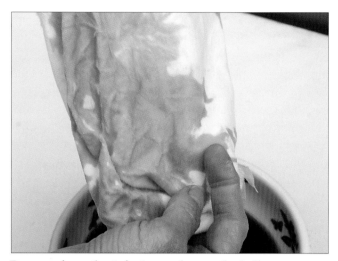

Remove from the infusion and open the ball.

If you want it a little darker, crumple the velvet into a ball again and re-dye it.

When it is the shade you like, lay flat to dry. Press face-down to remove some of the wrinkles.

## SEA SPONGE METHOD

Lay the velvet on a flat surface. Dip the sea sponge into the tea infusion.

Dip the sponge into the tea infusion again and reapply to the velvet surface. If you wait a few minutes and apply the sponge overlapping the edge of an area already dyed, it will create a darker area and give a hard edge to the area being overdyed.

Leave the velvet lying flat to dry.

Sponge the tea onto the velvet surface, moving the sponge to different areas of the velvet.

Compare the differences between the two styles of dyeing.

The straight grain of the velvet can become torqued when being torn.

If you have overcorrected the grain, gently stretch the fabric in the opposite direction by taking hold of the top left and lower right corners.

To straighten the grain, grasp the top right and lower left corners between your thumbs and forefingers and gently pull. Release your grip on the velvet and check to see if it has straightened out. If not, stretch again in the same manner and check for straightness.

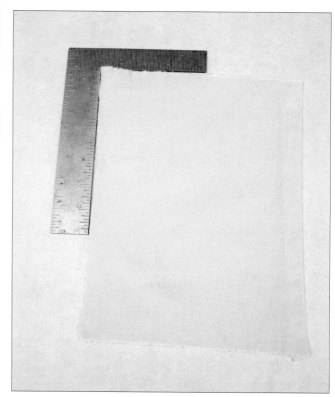

Once the grain has been corrected properly, you can mount the velvet and start your painting.

First cut a piece of Crescent Perfect Mount board the exact size of the drawing. Do not yet remove the paper backing. Before cutting the velvet, you must determine the direction of the nap of the material.

Here are two pieces of velvet shown with the grain running in opposite directions. Will your painting be longer horizontally or vertically?

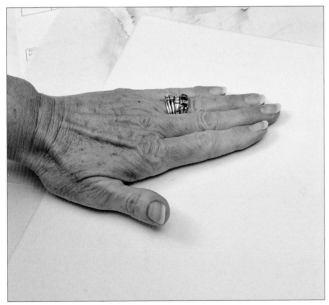

The nap of the velvet should always be smooth to the touch when you run your fingers across the material from what will be the top to the bottom of the painting. If it feels rough, turn the material until the nap feels soft and smooth when moving your fingers from top to bottom.

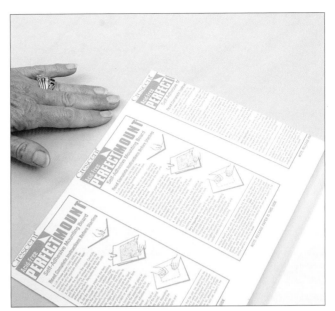

Place the velvet on the table to accommodate this view of your finished theorem.

If you are cutting a smaller portion from a large piece of velvet to use for your painting, first lay the mounting board on the velvet in the direction of the finished painting.

Then cut the velvet around the mounting board, leaving an extra $1/2$ inch of material on each side.

Now carefully turn the velvet over so that the nap direction remains the same.

Center the mounting board on the wrong side of the velvet, sticky side down.

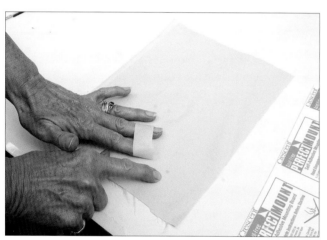

Remove any lint from the wrong side of the fabric with masking tape.

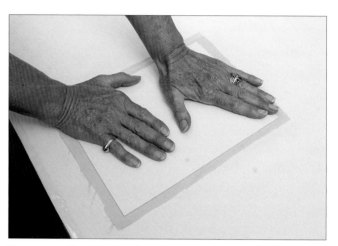

Press your hand over the mounting board to secure it to the fabric.

Next, remove the protective sheet from the sticky side of the mounting board, saving it to cover your painting later until you are able to frame it.

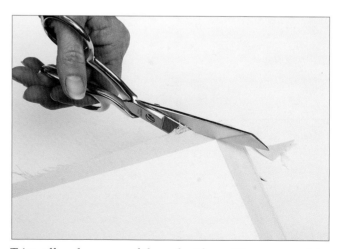

Trim off each corner of the velvet by cutting away a triangular piece not covered by the mounting board.

Run a bead of pH-neutral glue along the edge of the board.

Then fold over the edges of the velvet onto the board, pressing lightly to glue them in place. If the glue should get on the right side of the velvet, it will not come out and will permanently ruin the nap, so take care not to get glue on the table surface or your fingers, and keep a damp paper towel on hand to wipe them clean.

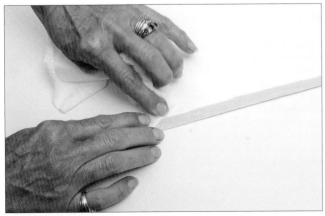

With a dry paper towel, blot any excess glue in the mitered corners. Let the glue set up and dry.

Finally, turn the mounted board over so that the right side of the velvet is up.

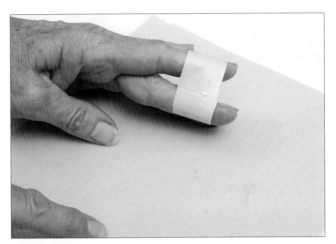

With a little piece of masking tape, remove any lint pieces from the velvet surface.

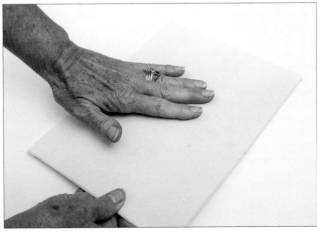

Again check to see that the nap is running correctly before beginning to paint.

## Protecting the Velvet When Storing Mounted Boards

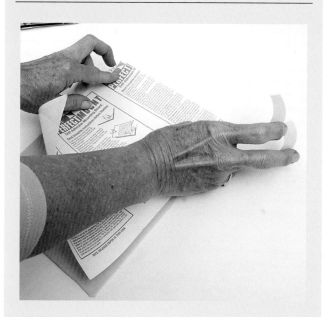

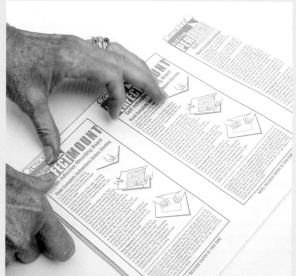

If you are not going to paint your theorem right away, put the protective backing sheet over the velvet and tape the four corners to hold it in place. This will keep the velvet clean until you are ready to paint.

### CUTTING MULTIPLES OF ONE SIZE

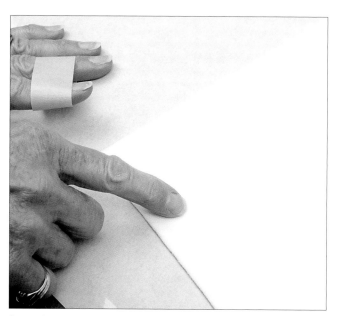

Sometimes it is more economical to tear your velvet into strips rather than cut it from the yard of fabric piece by piece. You can get five vertical or four horizontal theorems out of 52-inch-wide material, with an extra piece left over for some small paintings. Lay a velvet board along the selvage edge of the material, and clip the velvet in from the edge about an inch. Remove the velvet board and set aside. Grasp the fabric with both hands and quickly tear. This will create additional lint. Shake most of it off outside, then use masking tape to remove the rest. Lay the strip of velvet on the table. Place the mounting board on the velvet and cut the velvet strip into pieces. Move the mounting board after each piece is cut.

When mixing colors for your paintings, it is important to add only very small amounts of other paints to the base color. In the patterns, the first color listed is the base color. A lesser amount of the next color is added, and then a smaller amount of each subsequent color. Mix each into the base color well before adding the next one. (Refer to Perfect Palette on page 62.)

Use the flat of the palette knife, and not the tip, to mix the colors with a rotating, mashing motion. It is very important to thoroughly mix the paints before using them. The Canton Bowl of Cherries and Apricots pattern again will serve as an example.

You will use three palette sheets. Remove two sheets from the palette tablet on which to mix your colors.

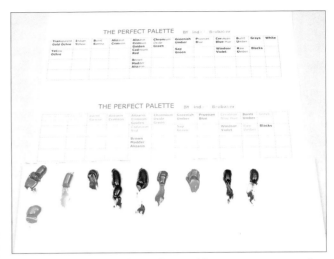

On a clean sheet on the palette tablet, create your main palette by putting on it all the colors listed at the beginning of the pattern for the Canton Bowl. Now you will start mixing your colors. After each one is mixed, you will place it on your main palette near the color that most closely resembles it. The first colors you will mix are for the apricots. Start by mixing three different yellows, ranging from a soft yellow to a peachy color

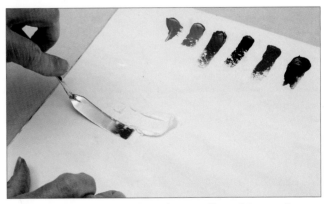

Place a quarter-size dollop of Permalba white on the loose palette sheet. Add increasingly smaller amounts of the following colors to the white, cleaning your palette knife before each new color as pictured on the next page:

yellow ochre,

Indian yellow,

and transparent gold ochre. Mix well after each addition.

Divide the soft yellow that has resulted into three parts. Leave the first portion as is.

To the second portion, add a small amount of Grumbacher red.

Then add some raw umber. This second color should wind up a peachy yellow.

To the third portion, also add a small amount of Grumbacher red. Mix well.

Then add a touch of alizarin crimson golden. Adjust as necessary to match the color shown here.

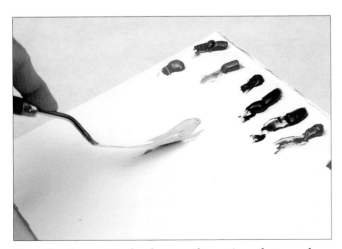

Place the three mixed colors on the main palette under the yellow section of the Perfect Palette, keeping the colors light to dark. Then, discard this palette sheet.

With your palette knife, remove some alizarin crimson from the main palette and place on the left side of the other palette sheet.

Pick up some Prussian blue and place this above the alizarin crimson.

Mix some of the Prussian blue into the alizarin crimson to create a deep cherry red. Mix well. Add a little more blue if necessary, but be careful not to make a purple. Place this mixed color on the main palette under the reds.

Remove some raw umber from the main palette and place it on the right side of the palette sheet. Repeat with Prussian blue.

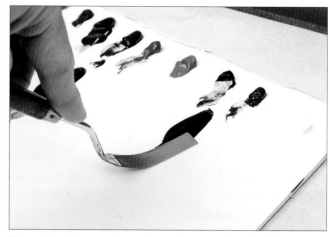

Place this blue on the main palette under the blue section.

Mix some raw umber into the Prussian blue, creating a deep greenish blue.

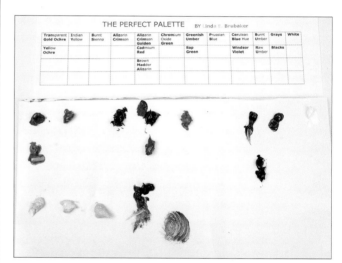

Once the colors have been mixed and placed on the main palette, proceed with the painting.

Before placing the stencil on the velvet, check that the grain has a smooth feel when you run your hand from top to bottom. Then remove any loose threads or lint with masking tape.

Place the first stencil on the mounted velvet board. Tape the stencil at the top two corners.

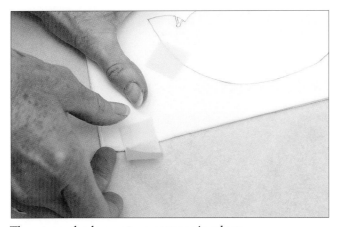

Then tape the lower two corners in place.

If the stencil is slightly longer than the velvet board, trim off the bottom to fit.

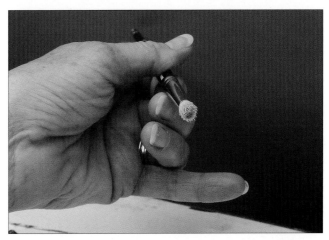

Pick up a small amount of paint on the center of the stencil brush. I will be demonstrating with a variety of colors. It is important to use a different stencil brush for each color.

Distribute the paint evenly through the stencil brush by swirling it on your palette directly under the color you have used. In theorem painting, "less is best" when loading the stencil brush for painting. More paint can be added later if needed. Before painting on the velvet exposed through the stencil opening, test the loaded brush on a paper towel or scrap of velvet to check that it is not too full of paint and that the paint is evenly distributed in the brush.

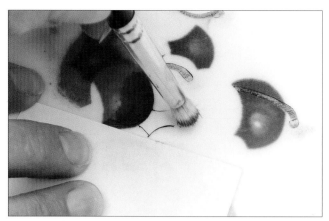

Use shields to cover items not being painted at this time.

Gently brush the velvet with the paint-loaded stencil brush, starting at the top of the opening of the stencil and moving to the right and downward. It is always best to start painting at the top of the pattern so as not to smear paint with your hand or arm as you move down the pattern from one stencil opening to the next.

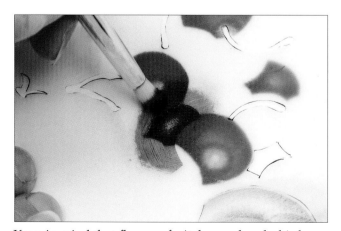

Keep in mind that flowers, fruit, leaves, bowls, birds, and butterflies have curved surfaces and should be round in appearance.

Do not brush the velvet from bottom to top, however. This would create a ruffed surface on the velvet and cause the painting to lose its realism and smooth appearance. Paint all items on the first stencil. Then remove this stencil and place the second one into position.

If there are areas on subsequent stencils that do not match up and spaces are left between the items, trace a line on the area of the stencil that needs to be corrected.

Remove the stencil and trim the opening to this line.

Replace the stencil and continue painting the theorem. Always place shields over open stencil areas that are not being painted.

If a stencil opening has been cut too large and a previously painted item extends into the opening of the next stencil, use a shield to cover the area. When you are finished painting all the stencils, it is now time to paint the fine lines.

## Painting Tips

• Make sure the nap of the velvet is going in the right direction. Velvet is like the fur on a cat or dog. Petting the animal from head to tail feels very smooth and soft. But if you pet the animal from the tail to the head, you will meet resistance. The same holds true with velvet.

• Shading is critical and can make or break a theorem. Many of the lovely old theorems had subtle shading.

• Use the Perfect Palette (page 62), which will help you learn the colors.

• Place small amounts of paint on your palette, and only in the colors you will use on this painting. The "less is best" rule applies here too.

• Use one stencil brush per color.

• Pick up a small amount of paint on the center of the brush.

• Arrange the brushes on your table in the same way the paint is arranged on the Perfect Palette. This will help keep you from mixing up the colors in the brushes.

• It is easy to add more color to the theorem but impossible to lighten the color. Again the guideline "less is best" applies.

• Test the brush loaded with color on a paper towel or scrap of velvet. If the paint is not evenly distributed in the bristles, it will create a blotch (left) on the item being painted, and this is usually difficult to cover with subsequent shading.

• Brush, rather than dab, the color onto the velvet.

• Brush the velvet only from top to bottom, side to side, or on the diagonal going top to bottom. Never brush from bottom to top. This would roughen the velvet, and if this occurs, it will never become smooth again.

• Learn to control the brush. Make the brush work for you and not vice versa.

Fine lines are painted with oil paints to which Turpenoid is added to create a watery mixture on the palette.

Practice scrolls and tendrils on a paper towel or scrap piece of velvet before you do the fine linework on your painting. Practice signing your name on a paper towel with the watery Turpenoid–oil paint mixture.

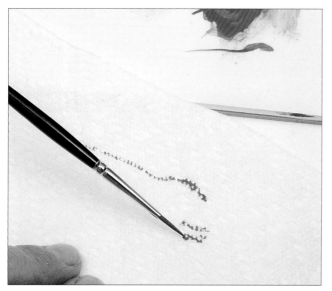

To keep this watery mixture from making thick lines on your painting, first drag the liner brush—while rolling it at the same time—across a paper towel. This action also reestablishes the point on the brush.

Then practice writing your name with the mixture on a scrap of velvet with the liner brush.

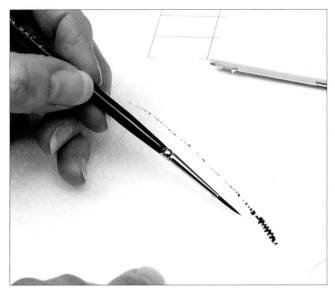

There are times when the Turpenoid–oil paint mixture will bleed into the velvet or paper towel. This usually happens when Prussian blue is used in the mixture.

If you are called away and want to keep your paint from drying out, cover your palette with clear plastic wrap. The colors will be fine to use the next day. If you find you cannot finish your theorem and may not be able to return to work on it for several days, wrap your paints in clear plastic wrap and place them in the freezer. When you are ready to begin painting again, remove from the freezer and thaw for a few minutes.

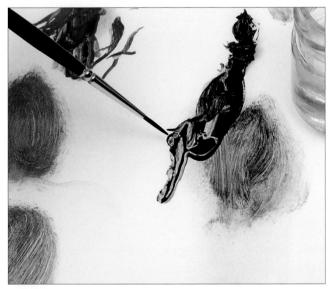

To prevent this when using a Turpenoid–Prussian blue mixture, add a drop of Avon Skin So Soft oil. It will slow down the wicking of the paint into the velvet so that you get thin, crisp lines. Do not use Skin So Soft with all linework, however.

If you drop a brush onto your theorem or make a mistake such as painting a leaf where a flower petal should have been painted, you can correct the error by washing the problem area with Murphy's Oil Soap. The first time you use this process, it can be unsettling.

There are times when this process does not remove the color completely, especially when the error involves Prussian blue paint. Not only can this color be stubborn to remove, but it also has a habit of getting everywhere when released from the paint tube, so take extra care when using it. To correct painting mistakes, use the following procedure.

Carefully loosen the glued edge of velvet from the back of the mounting board.

Then, while taking great care, peel the velvet from the mounting board, making sure the wet paint on the front does not brush against another area. If it does and paint is smudged, you will have to wash this out too.

Now wet the velvet with cold water. Gently brush some Murphy's Oil Soap over the wet velvet with the pad of your finger, brushing with the grain of the velvet. The oil soap will dissolve the oil paint.

During the cleaning process, some other areas of the paint will be dissolved by the Murphy's Oil Soap as the soap leaches through the wet velvet. Do not be too concerned about this.

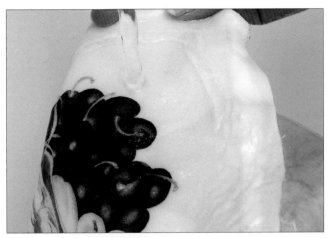

Rinse with cold running water. Apply some more Murphy's Oil Soap, and rinse again with cold running water until all the paint is removed.

Turn the painting upside down and rinse again to make sure all the soap is removed.

Lay the painted velvet on a towel to dry completely; it will take twelve to twenty-four hours.

When the velvet is fully dry, lay the painting facedown on a clean surface.

## Quick-Fix Tip for Removing Mistakes

There are times when you are close to finishing the painting and make a mistake. All is not lost. The mistake can be corrected with the following procedure:

Wet a cotton swab with water, and gently dab the water onto the area to be cleaned. Dip another cotton swab into some Murphy's Oil Soap, and gently dab the soap onto the wetted mistake. Blot with a clean paper towel. Wet the area again with clean water, and blot with a clean part of the paper towel. Apply more Murphy's Oil Soap if needed, and blot again with a clean paper towel. Then add more clean water with the cotton swab and blot with a clean paper towel. Rinse several more times with the cotton swab and blot. Before repainting the area, leave the velvet completely dry, normally two to six hours. Then finish the painting. This process will leave behind a watermark on the velvet. To eliminate the watermark, remove the velvet from the board, rinse thoroughly with water, and dry flat. Then remount the velvet.

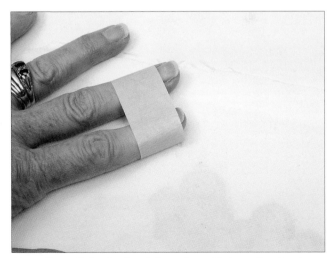

Clean lint off the back of the velvet. If the adhesive has peeled off the board, cut a new piece of mounting board in the size needed.

Center the sticky side of the mounting board on the back of the velvet painting; then gently press the center of the board.

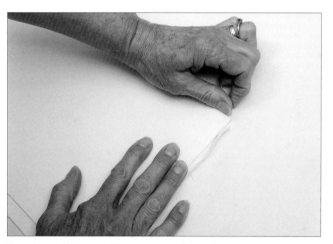

Starting with the sides, stretch the velvet painting to fold the edges of the fabric over the edges of the board as before.

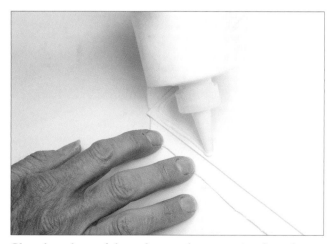

Glue the edges of the velvet to the mounting board.

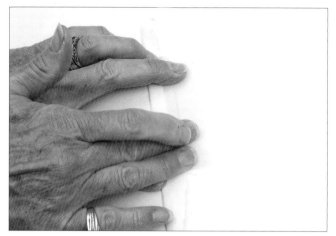

When regluing the velvet to the board, sometimes the velvet will not stick, so place some tape to hold the edges in place until the glue dries.

## REMOVING LINEWORK

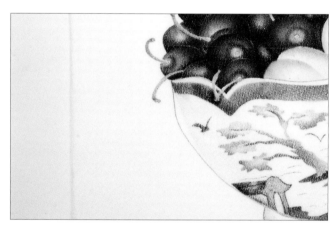

Removing linework is more difficult and requires more attention. Start by removing the velvet from the backing board, following the above instructions. Then wet the velvet as above.

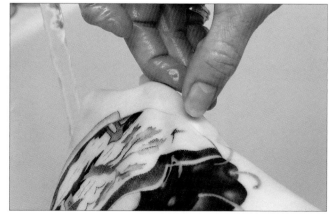

Dip your finger into the Murphy's Oil Soap and touch the soap to the area needing to be cleaned.

With the pad of your finger, gently brush the soap over the wet velvet, going with the grain.

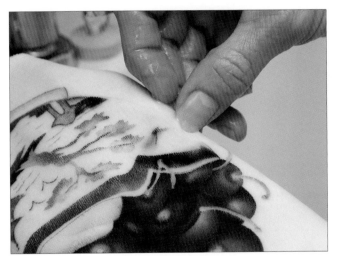

Use the flat of your fingernail to remove stubborn lines, again gently rubbing with the grain of the fabric.

Rinse well with running water.

Turn the painting so the back of the velvet is facing up and the affected area is in your hand. Reapply the Murphy's Oil Soap to the back of the painting. With the edge of your fingernail, rub the offending line in the direction of the grain of the fabric. Rinse well with running water. Repeat with additional Murphy's Oil Soap if necessary and rinse well. Sometimes the line will not be completely removed, but it will not be very noticeable. Lay the painted velvet on a towel to dry. Remount the velvet as in the steps above.

Now you are ready to repaint the problem areas as necessary with the following steps.

Place the stencil required to fix the problem on the painting, lining up the design as best you can. Uncover your saved paints.

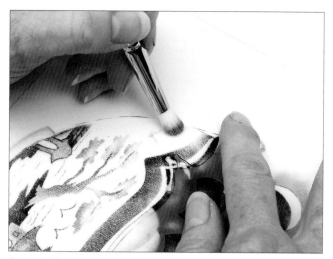

Cover all areas not being painted with shields, and carefully paint onto the original painting.

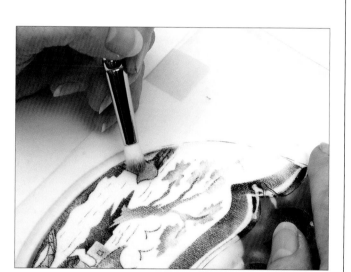

Shift the stencil as necessary to line up with the previously painted areas.

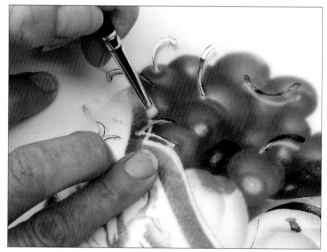

Repaint all areas needed.

Here is the completed restenciled theorem.

Finally, repaint all linework to complete the painting.

When you are finished using your brushes for the day, it is very important to clean them. Liner brushes come with protective plastic sleeves. Save these sleeves so that you can replace them after the brush is cleaned.

The best and quickest way to clean brushes is with the use of solvent. First pour a little Turpenoid into a small bottle. Immediately clean your liner brush by dipping it in Turpenoid and stroking across a paper towel. Do not swish the brush in the solvent or rub on the bottom of the jar. These actions are hard on all brushes and also make the Turpenoid dirty.

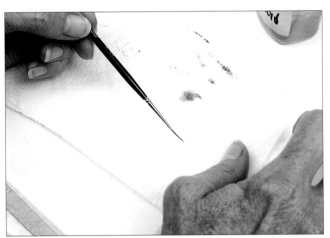

Dip and stroke repeatedly until all color is removed from the liner brush. Do not use soap and water on this brush.

After the color is completely removed, dip the liner brush in Skin So Soft oil.

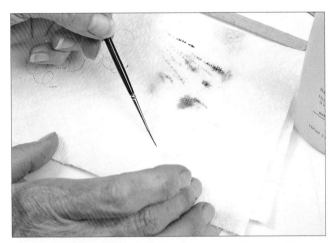

Then pull the brush across a paper towel in one direction while rolling the bristles to reestablish the point.

Now carefully replace the protective sleeve that originally came on the liner brush. Never leave any brush sit in a solvent; it will ruin the bristles.

Next, clean each of the stencil brushes one at a time. Dip into the small jar of Turpenoid, and then swirl the diluted pigment onto a paper towel.

Wash your stencil brushes with any brand of liquid laundry soap. You can knead the soap into the bristles with your fingers or use an inexpensive brush-cleaning pad from a craft or art store.

Repeat dipping and swirling until all color is removed from the brush.

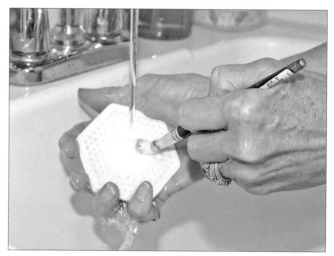

Rinse well with water. Lay the stencil brushes on a paper towel to dry.

# Basic Painting Exercises

This copy of an antique theorem is a good example of all the basic painting techniques taught in this chapter. Try these exercises before beginning the patterns that follow. You can frame your results or sew them into little pincushions.

All these designs are for a velvet board measuring 4 x 4 inches. Trace and cut the designs, and mount the velvet onto 4 x 4-inch pieces of mounting board. You might want to stencil all the designs first before painting the detail. This will give you extensive practice first with the stenciling technique, and then with the liner brush. For multi-stencil paintings, note that each stencil is always painted and removed before the next stencil in the sequence is placed.

## Perfect Palette

I developed what I call the "Perfect Palette" many years ago when I began painting theorems. I was having difficulty distinguishing the different pigments from each other, so I began to place the paints in a certain order on my palette. This order not only will help you remember the colors, but also avoid mixing colors unintentionally. You need to make a conscious effort to put the paints in this order and to distribute the paint evenly in the stencil brush below that color on your palette. Make several copies of this paint order to be used at the top of each palette until you have memorized the colors. If you want to add another color that is not listed on the Perfect Palette, place it farther down toward, but not in, the center of your palette. Always keep like colors together—the yellows in one section, the reds in another section, and so forth. For example, if you want to add ultramarine blue, place it under the cerulean blue section.

### PALETTE
- transparent gold ochre
- yellow ochre
- Indian yellow
- burnt sienna
- alizarin crimson
- alizarin crimson golden
- chromium oxide green
- Prussian blue
- cerulean blue
- burnt umber
- Davy's gray

Add more colors as needed, following the Perfect Palette.

| Transparent Gold Ochre | Indian Yellow | Burnt Sienna | Alizarin Crimson | Alizarin Crimson Golden | Chromium Oxide Green | Greenish Umber | Prussian Blue | Cerulean Blue | Burnt Umber | Grays | White |
|---|---|---|---|---|---|---|---|---|---|---|---|
| Yellow Ochre | | | | Cadmium Red | | Sap Green | | Winsor Violet | Raw Umber | Blacks | |
| | | | | Brown Madder Alizarin | | | | | | | |
| | | | | | | | | | | | |

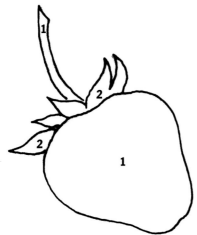

The strawberry is one of the easiest fruits to paint. Usually it is painted with one color. Later, you might want to experiment with undertones of yellow and leaving some white areas at the base or hull.

## Stencil Number 1

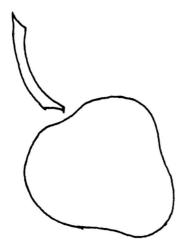

**Stencil Number 1**. With a large stencil brush, pick up a small amount of alizarin crimson golden. Distribute the color evenly in the bristles by swirling directly under the same color on your palette.

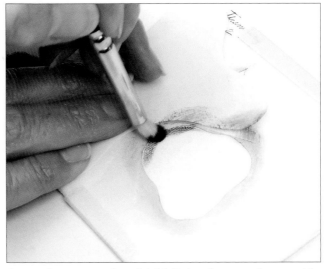

Cover the stem with a shield. Paint the strawberry with the alizarin crimson golden.

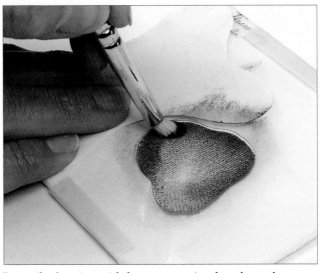

Paint the berries with long, sweeping brush strokes, keeping the strokes curved.

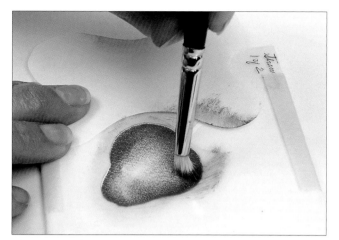

The outer edges of the berry should be darker than the center.

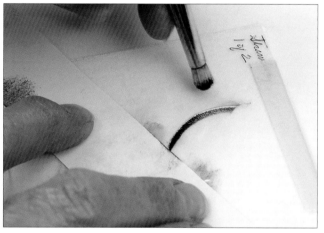

Move the shield to cover the berry. With a new brush, pick up some yellow ochre, and distribute the color evenly in the bristles as you did for the first color. Paint the stem with the yellow ochre. With another brush, pick up some chromium oxide green, and again distribute the color evenly in the bristles. Shade the stem with the chromium oxide green along one edge, and fade toward the other edge to create a curved appearance.

**Stencil Number 2**

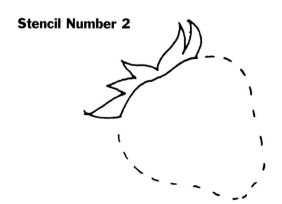

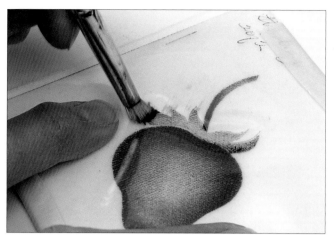

**Stencil Number 2.** Paint the hull of the strawberry with yellow ochre.

Shade the hull with chromium oxide green.

**Detail.** With a palette knife, mix some alizarin crimson golden with a little burnt umber on your palette. Add some Turpenoid to the resulting brownish red to create a watery mixture. Then use the liner brush with this mixture to paint some dots on the strawberry to represent seeds.

Both the pear and the apple are created by layering and blending colors. You layer colors on top of one another, and then blend the edges so that there is a gentle transition between them.

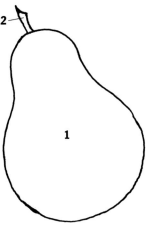

Pears are similar in shape to the figure eight. Keep this in mind when painting this fruit.

**Stencil Number 1**

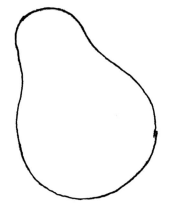

**Stencil Number 1.** Use a new brush to pick up a small amount of Indian yellow, and distribute the color evenly in the bristles by swirling directly under the same color on your palette.

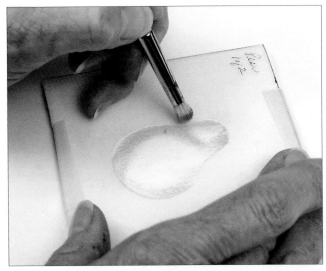

Base-paint the pear with the Indian yellow, keeping the edges a deeper value of the yellow. Paint the curve of the pear across the center with the yellow.

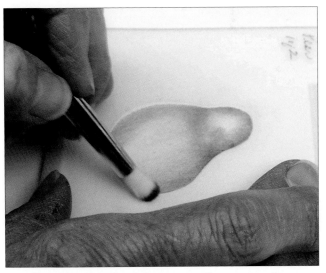

Using another brush, pick up a small amount of transparent gold ochre, and distribute the color evenly in the bristles as before. Shade the edges and the curve on the center of the pear with the transparent gold ochre.

With a fresh brush, pick up a small amount of burnt si-enna, and swirl to distribute the color: It's not necessary to repeat all this in every step. I'm shortening it in the future to just "and swirl" or "and distribute it evenly in the bristles." Shade the edges and the curve on the center of the pear with the burnt sienna.

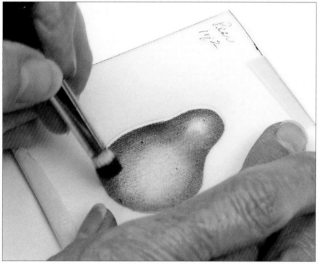

Using yet another brush, pick up a small amount of alizarin crimson and swirl. Shade the pear on the left side with a light blush of alizarin crimson.

**Stencil Number 2**

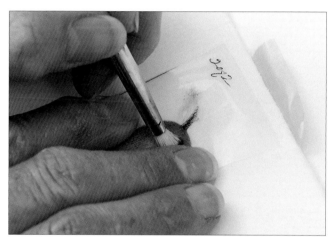

**Stencil Number 2**. Pick up a small amount of burnt sienna and swirl. Paint the stem with burnt sienna.

**Detail**. Mix some Turpenoid into a small amount of burnt sienna on your palette to create a watery mixture. Then use the liner brush with this mixture to paint a small curvy line at the bottom of the pear to represent the blossom end.

**Stencil Number 1.** Place the half of the curve with the dip at the bottom of the stem. Paint some Indian yellow along the lower portion of the stem and at the center of the curve.

Cut the curve for the stem of the apple. Save both pieces of the curve.

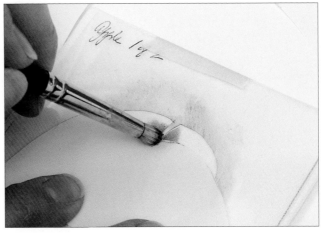

Add a little chromium oxide green on top of the yellow at the base of the stem.

## Stencil Number 1

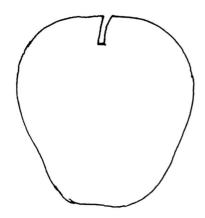

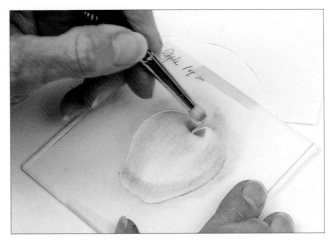

Remove the curve, and paint a light coat of Indian yellow on the rest of the apple.

Place the half of the curve containing the bump over the stem, lining up the edge of the curve with the edge of the painted yellow curve.

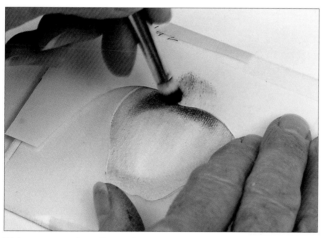

Using a new brush, pick up a small amount of alizarin crimson, and distribute it evenly in the bristles.

Paint some red along the edge of the curve, fading out toward the edge.

Remove the curve, and paint the rest of the apple with alizarin crimson.

Shade the edges of the apple with a darker red, keeping the center lighter.

**Stencil Number 2**

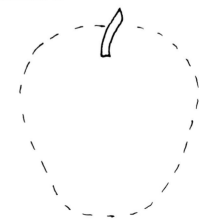

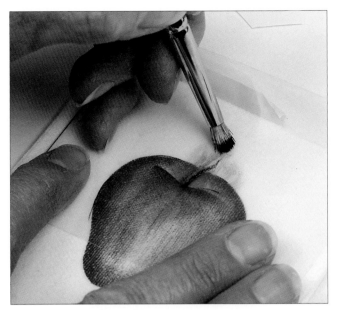

**Detail**. There is no detail on this project, other than signing your name.

**Stencil Number 2**. With a new brush, pick up some burnt sienna and swirl. Paint the stem with this color, keeping the edges darker.

# Peach

The steps for painting the peach and the plum not only reemphasize the blending of colors, but also teach two different methods.

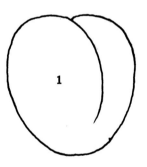

Place a scrap of stencil film over the drawing, and trace the curve of the peach. Cut this curve. You will be using the half of the curve that is concave.

**Stencil Number 1**

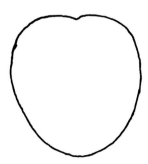

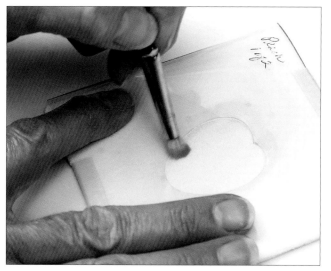

**Stencil Number 1**. Use a new brush to pick up a small amount of Indian yellow, and distribute the color evenly in the bristles by swirling directly under the same color on your palette. Base-paint the peach with the Indian yellow, making the edges a deeper value of the yellow. Place the concave curve on the peach, aligning the curve with the point in the top of the peach. Paint along this curve with Indian yellow. Then remove the curve.

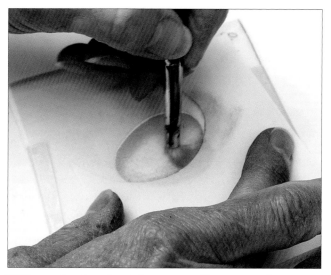

With another brush, pick up a small amount of transparent gold ochre on the brush and distribute the color in the bristles. Shade the edges of the peach with this color.

Replace the curve on the peach, again aligning the curve with the point in the top of the peach. Paint along this curve with the transparent gold ochre, blending the two yellows.

Remove the curve.

Use yet another new brush to pick up a small amount of alizarin crimson golden and swirl. Shade the edges of the peach with this color, blending the red into the yellows. Then replace the curve on the peach, aligning the same way. Paint along this curve with the alizarin crimson golden, blending into the two yellows. Remove the curve.

**Detail**. This project has no detail, other than signing your name.

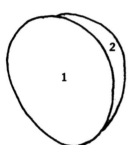

**Stencil Number 1**

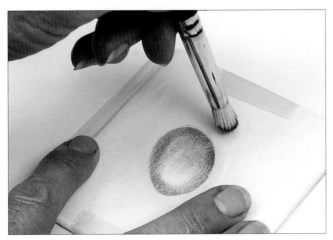

**Stencil Number 1**: Base-paint the plum with alizarin crimson, shading a darker value along the edges.

Using a new brush loaded with Prussian blue, shade the plum, starting along the edges and working toward the center. If some colored fuzz develops while painting, gently press a piece of masking tape onto the fuzz and remove.

Complete the shading with Prussian blue on the plum.

**Stencil Number 2**

**Stencil Number 2**. With alizarin crimson, start at the outer edge and paint toward the other half of the plum. Fade the red to the white of the velvet.

Shade over top of the red paint with Prussian blue, again fading out to the white velvet.

On both the daisy and the morning glory, you will learn how to fade the color to the natural color of the velvet. There should be no hard line between the stronger color on the edge and the velvet color, just a gradual fading.

The daisy design teaches about shadows. Look at the drawing and determine which petal is behind the one next to it. Imagine where the shadow is. Place the color along one side and then the tip of each petal, fading to the white of the velvet. Keep the color close to the side of the petal.

**Stencil Number 1**

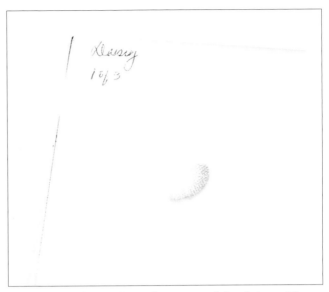

**Stencil Number 1**. Paint the center of the daisy with Indian yellow.

Shade the lower half of the center of the daisy along the lower edge with transparent gold ochre.

## Stencil Number 2

**Stencil Number 2**. Use a shield between the petals.

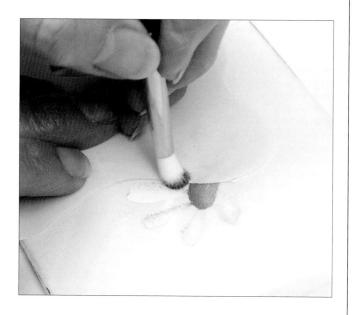

Paint along the right side and the tip of each daisy petal with Davy's gray. *Note*: Some colors do not show up well when stenciling, but when the stencil is removed, they are darker than you think. Davy's gray is one of those colors.

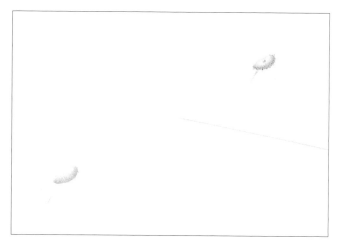

## Stencil Number 3

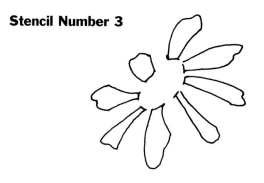

**Stencil Number 3**. As you can see, the lower petal in the center is lightly shaded on each side. Keep this paint very light. On the petals to the left of the center petal, shade the right side and around the tip of each petal with Davy's gray. This will create the shadow found naturally in a daisy.

74

Shade the petals to the right of the center petal on the left side with Davy's gray.

**Detail**. To give the yellow flower center depth, paint a pale green dot in the middle with your smallest stencil brush. To do this, use just the tip of the smallest stencil brush to pick up paint from the area where you swirled your large brush to distribute the chromium oxide green earlier. Very little paint is needed. Touch the tip of the brush in the center of the daisy and rotate one complete turn. This is plenty of green.

With Turpenoid mixed with some burnt sienna, use the liner brush to place dots along the edge of the flower center, starting at the top right and following along the center and the petals. Paint two or three rows of random dots between the petals and the center. Then paint a semicircle around the lower half of the green dot in the center.

# Morning Glories

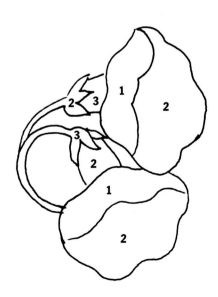

**Stencil Number 1**

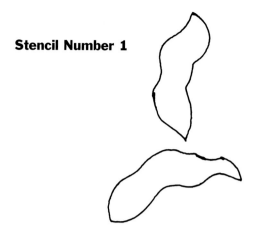

**Stencil Number 1**. Pick up a dot of Prussian blue on the tip of your stencil brush, and distribute the paint evenly in the brush by swirling it directly under the same color on the palette.

Use a shield to cover the right flower. Paint the left petal, starting on the right side and leaving some of the white velvet exposed in the center of the petal. Shade the left side of the petal along the edge, keeping this side light in value. To leave the center light, use less pressure on your brush and lift it up and off the velvet, fading the blue to the white of the velvet.

Test the amount of paint in the brush by brushing it on a paper towel or scrap of velvet before starting to paint the morning glories.

Repeat this on the other petal. Then remove the first stencil.

**Stencil Number 2**

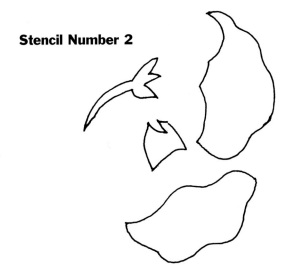

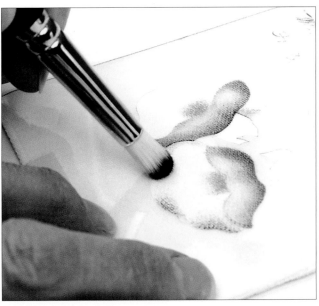

Paint the Indian yellow along the edge in the middle only of the petal, next to the blue area painted on the previous stencil.

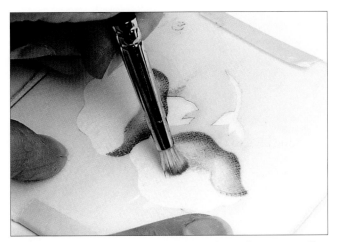

**Stencil Number 2**. Using a new brush, pick up a small amount of Indian yellow and distribute the paint evenly.

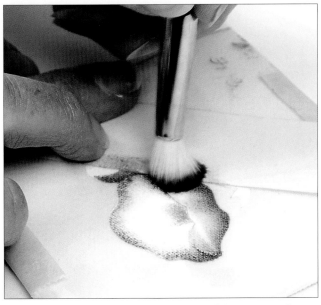

With the blue brush, which should still have enough paint in it, paint some blue on the outer edge of the stencil (the area opposite the yellow). Shade the blue toward the center, leaving white showing near the yellow. If the blue and yellow mix, it will turn the center green.

Cover the calyx and stem with a shield before beginning to paint.

Paint Prussian blue along both edges of the trumpet area of the morning glory.

Using a new brush, paint the calyx and stem with yellow ochre. With another brush, shade the calyx and stem with chromium oxide green.

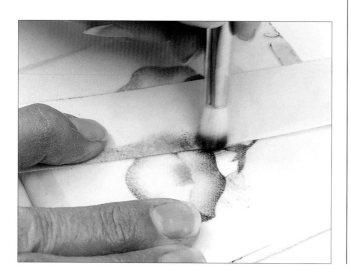

**Stencil Number 3**

**Stencil Number 3**. Cover the calyx and stem with a shield. Paint Prussian blue along both edges of the trumpet area of the morning glory.

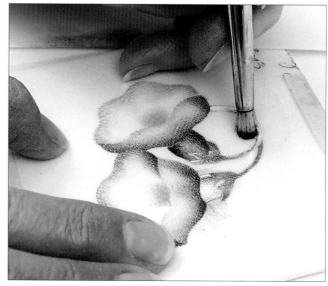

Paint the calyx and stem with yellow ochre, then shade these areas with chromium oxide green.

**Detail**. Add Turpenoid to some yellow ochre to make a watery mixture. With the liner brush, paint some dots near the blue in the yellow area of the morning glory.

78

When painting the forget-me-nots and the following two designs—roses and currants—you will learn about shadowing, the interaction of multiple petals, and rendering clusters of flowers and fruits. The areas of a petal or berry that are shadowed by another petal, berry, or a leaf in front of it are always a deeper value and should be shaded darker.

**Stencil Number 1**

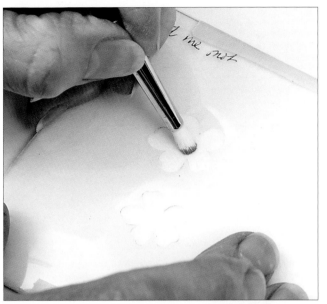

**Stencil Number 1**. Use a number 1 Scharff round scrubber with a small amount of Indian yellow to paint a little circle in the center of each flower, rotating the brush as you did with the green in the center of the daisy. Keep the yellow confined to the center; if it mixes with the blue you paint next, you will get green.

With a new brush, pick up some cerulean blue and distribute it evenly by swirling, as in the earlier projects.

Place a shield between each flower.

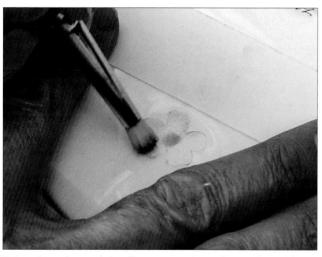

Paint the edges of the flower petals with cerulean blue. Fade the blue into the yellow, leaving a little white in between.

### Stencil Number 2

**Stencil Number 2.** Paint the center of the flower with the small brush loaded with Indian yellow. Paint the edges of the petals with cerulean blue.

Look at the pattern; shade the areas of the petals that are behind another flower a darker value of the cerulean blue.

**Stencil Number 3**

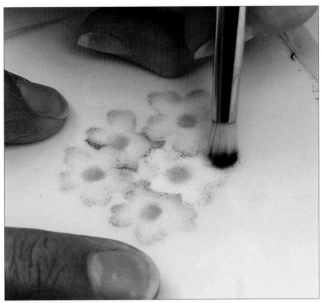

Paint the edges of the petals with cerulean blue. Look at the pattern, and shade the areas of the petals that are behind another flower a darker value of the cerulean blue.

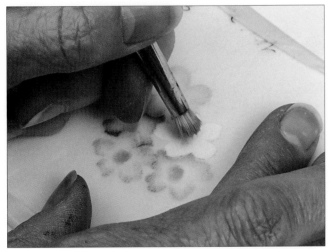

**Stencil Number 3**. With the small brush loaded with Indian yellow, paint the center of the flower.

**Detail**. Add Turpenoid to some alizarin crimson to make a watery mixture. With the liner brush, dot the center of the yellow area. Then add Turpenoid to some cerulean blue to make a second watery mixture. Use the liner brush to outline the flower.

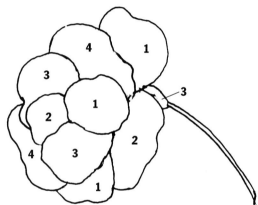

Look at the pattern to see where each petal is behind another.

**Stencil Number 1**

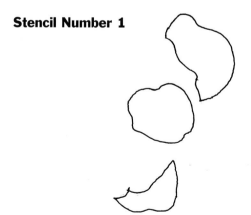

**Stencil Number 1**. Use a new brush, preferably a large one. It is easier to give depth to the petals with a larger brush than a small one. For this design, you need to place plenty of shields. Pick up a dot of alizarin crimson on the tip of your stencil brush, and swirl to distribute.

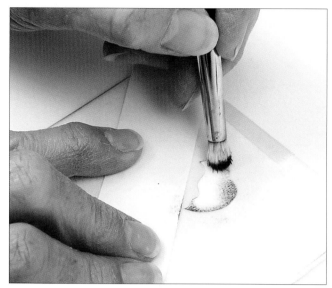

Cover the petals in the center and on the left with a shield. Paint the petal on the right with alizarin crimson, keeping the bottom of the petal darker. This is the area where the petal joins the stem.

Cover the left petal with a shield. Paint the center petal with the alizarin crimson, keeping the center a lighter red and using a darker value on the center bottom.

Cover the center petal, and shade the lower petal with alizarin crimson. Keep the part of the rose petal on the left darker along the straighter edge that attaches to the stem and is behind the other petals on the left.

**Stencil Number 2**

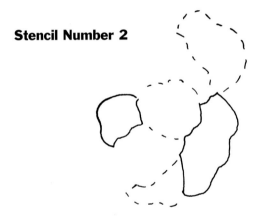

**Stencil Number 2**. Cover the left petal with a shield. Paint the right petal with alizarin crimson, keeping the area that is shadowed by other petals in front of it a deeper value.

Paint the right petal with alizarin crimson. Keep the area at the top of the petal a darker value. This is where the petal attaches to the stem.

**Stencil Number 3**

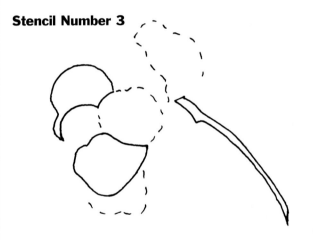

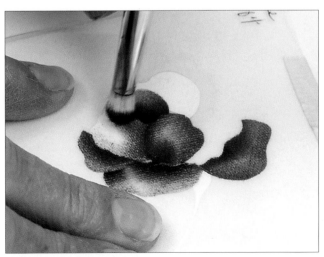

**Stencil Number 3**. With the alizarin crimson brush, paint the lower petal, keeping the area that is behind the center petal a deeper value.

Paint the other petal with alizarin crimson, keeping the area that is behind the petals in front of it a deeper value.

With another brush, paint the calyx and stem with yellow ochre. Then use a new brush to shade the stem with chromium oxide green.

**Stencil Number 4**

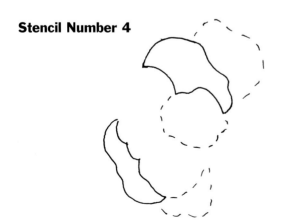

**Stencil Number 4**. With the alizarin crimson brush, paint the petal, keeping the area that is shadowed by other petals in front a deeper value.

Paint the lower petal, keeping the area that is shadowed by another petal in front a deeper value.

**Detail**. With some burnt sienna thinned with Turpenoid, paint some fine whiskers along the stem to represent thorns.

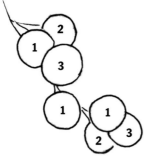

Using a palette knife, mix a small amount of burnt umber with some alizarin crimson to make a deep red on your palette.

**Stencil Number 1**

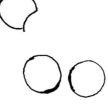

**Stencil Number 1**. With a new brush, pick up some of this alizarin crimson–burnt umber mixture and swirl to distribute. Starting with the berry on the left, paint the edges of the round currants with this mixture, keeping the center a light red. Make the concave edge a darker value. This is the part of the berry that is behind the others.

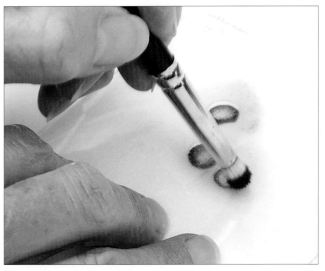

Paint the other round berries along the edges, keeping the centers a light red.

**Stencil Number 2**

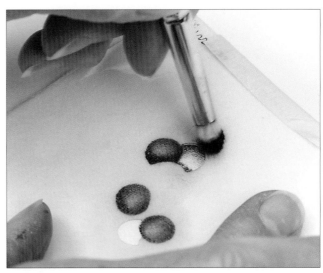

**Stencil Number 2**. Paint one of the berries with the alizarin crimson–burnt umber mixture, keeping the area of the currant that is behind another currant a darker value. Then paint the other berry the same way.

**Stencil Number 3**

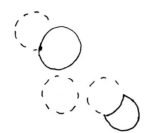

**Detail**. Add Turpenoid to some of the alizarin crimson–burnt umber paint to make a watery mixture. With the liner brush, paint fine curved lines on the currants, meeting in the center of the berries. Then add Turpenoid to some chromium oxide green to make a watery mixture. Use this to paint the stems with the liner brush, then sign your name.

**Stencil Number 3**. Paint one of the berries with the same alizarin crimson–burnt umber mixture, keeping the area of the currant that is behind another currant a darker value. Do the same for the other berry.

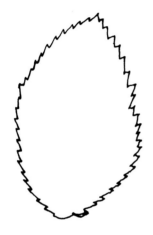

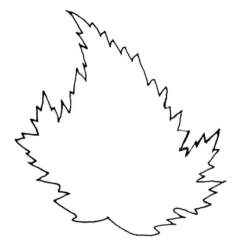

There are many ways to paint leaves. A good way to paint a realistic-looking leaf is with this one-two-three approach:

1. Start by base-painting the leaf in yellow ochre.
2. Load a new brush with burnt sienna and shade some of the edges. Do not shade the complete edge in burnt sienna, however, or it will look contrived.
3. Shade the leaf with chromium oxide green loaded on another brush. Be careful of the green. It is a very opaque color and can cover the brown tips, making them look muddy. Keep the leaf curved and not flat by making the center lighter than the edges.

**Curved leaves.** Another way to render a leaf is to add a curve in the center for a vein, which gives it added dimensions. Cut a curve out of an extra piece of stencil film to use on the leaf.

Begin by base-painting the leaf with yellow ochre.

With a new brush, paint some of the tips and edges with burnt sienna.

Begin to add a light coat of chromium oxide green to the leaf.

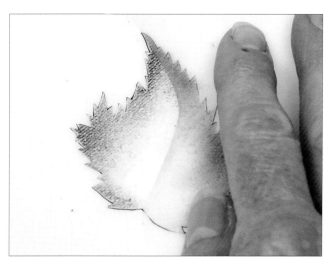

Place the curve in the center of the leaf.

Shade the exposed area with chromium oxide green.

Remove the curve, and paint the other side of the leaf.

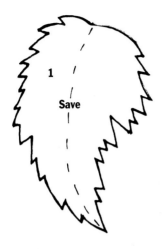

**Color variations**. Here is a third method with a different color variation. Save the leaf piece that was cut out from the stencil film. Draw a dotted line down the center, then cut the leaf in two. Base-paint the leaf with yellow ochre.

Place the left half of the cut-out leaf back into the stencil over the painted yellow leaf.

Secure the piece in place with masking tape.

Add a little more yellow ochre along the center edge of the replaced leaf cutout.

With a new brush, pick up a small amount of sap green and swirl.

Remove the leaf piece.

Start painting along the center and edges of the leaf with the sap green.

Paint the other half of the leaf with the sap green.

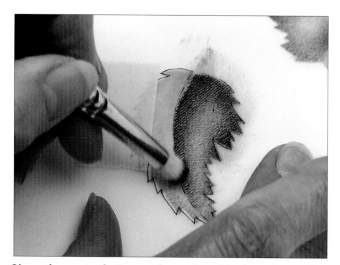

Keep the center between the replaced leaf section and the outer edge a lighter green.

**Turned leaves**. Turned leaves are painted by using two stencils for the same leaf.

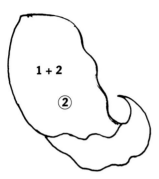

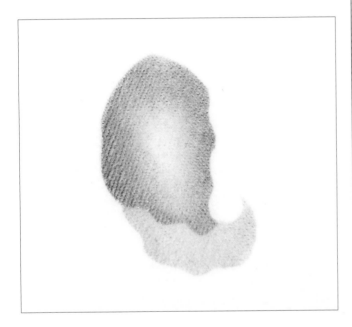

**Stencil Number 1**

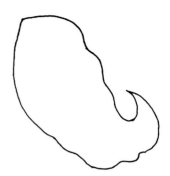

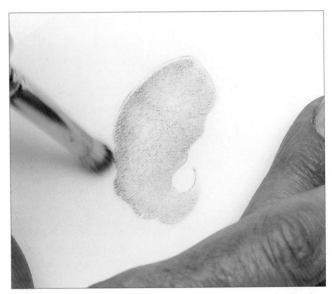

Place the first stencil on the velvet. Base-paint the leaf in yellow ochre.

Shade the leaf with chromium oxide green, keeping it very pale.

**Stencil Number 2**

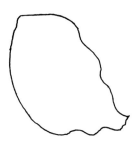

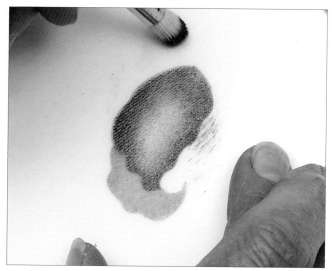

Shade along the remaining edges with the same color.

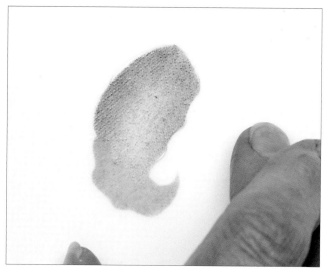

Remove the first stencil, and place the second on the leaf.

**Detail**. Add some greenish umber to the palette where shown on the Perfect Palette. With a palette knife, mix some greenish umber with some chromium oxide green on your palette. Add some Turpenoid to this dark green paint to create a watery mixture. Use a liner brush to paint the veins on all the leaves except the one painted with sap green. For that leaf, mix some sap green and some chromium oxide green on your palette with a palette knife. Add some Turpenoid to the deepened sap green paint to create a watery mixture. Then paint the veins on the leaf with a liner brush.

Shade along the lower edge of the leaf with chromium oxide green.

# Strawberry Wreath

This wreath theorem is a real winner that would make a wonderful gift for a special loved one or friend. The painting reinforces the basic techniques you have been learning, particularly in rendering the shadows created where one strawberry is behind another. Enlarge the design 106 percent to fit a 9 x 9-inch frame. Alternatively, you could make a pillow from the completed theorem. Read through each section of the instructions before beginning to paint. Refer to the painting sidebar on page 51.

## Palette

- yellow ochre
- burnt sienna
- alizarin crimson
- chromium oxide green
- greenish umber
- Davy's gray
- Turpenoid
- cadmium yellow acrylic paint for the blossom centers

**Stencil Number 1**

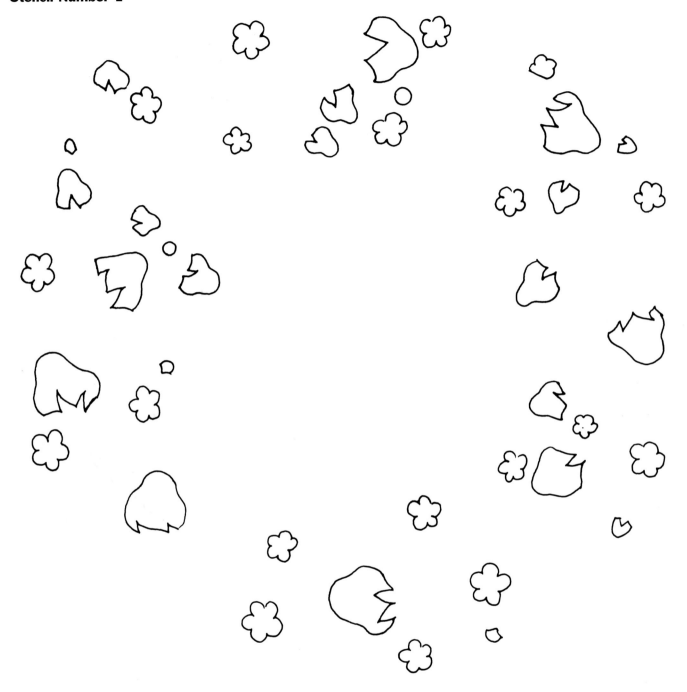

- **Blossoms and buds**. Paint the edges of the blossoms and buds with a very light application of Davy's gray.
- **Strawberries**. Base-paint the strawberries with alizarin crimson. Vary the color strength of the berries, because strawberries do not all have the same color value.

**Stencil Number 2**

- **Flower buds**. Paint the edges of the flower buds with a very light application of Davy's gray.
- **Strawberry hulls**. Base-paint the strawberry hulls with yellow ochre, then shade them with chromium oxide green along the edge of the stencil opening.
- **Leaves**. Base-paint the leaves with yellow ochre. Add a little burnt sienna here and there on the tips. Shade the leaves with chromium oxide green to give them a curvy shape.
- **Strawberries**. Base-paint the strawberries with alizarin crimson, again varying the depth of color. Where a berry is tucked behind another berry or a leaf, shade this area darker.

**Stencil Number 3**

- **Strawberry hulls**. Base-paint the hulls in yellow ochre, then shade with chromium oxide green along the edges of the stencil.
- **Leaves**. Base-paint the leaves in yellow ochre. Add a little burnt sienna to some of the tips. Shade in the leaves with chromium oxide green. Deepen areas that are behind another leaf or a berry.

97

**Stencil Number 4**

- **Leaves and strawberry hulls**. Base-paint the hulls with yellow ochre, then shade with chromium oxide green along the edges. Base-paint the leaves with yellow ochre. Add a little burnt sienna to some of the tips. Shade in the leaves with chromium oxide green. Deepen areas that are behind another leaf or a berry.

**DETAIL**
- **Blossoms and buds**. Make a grayed pink by mixing a touch of alizarin crimson with Davy's gray. Add Turpenoid. Outline each flower and bud with this color. On each bud, paint an undulating line in the center to give the appearance of petals.

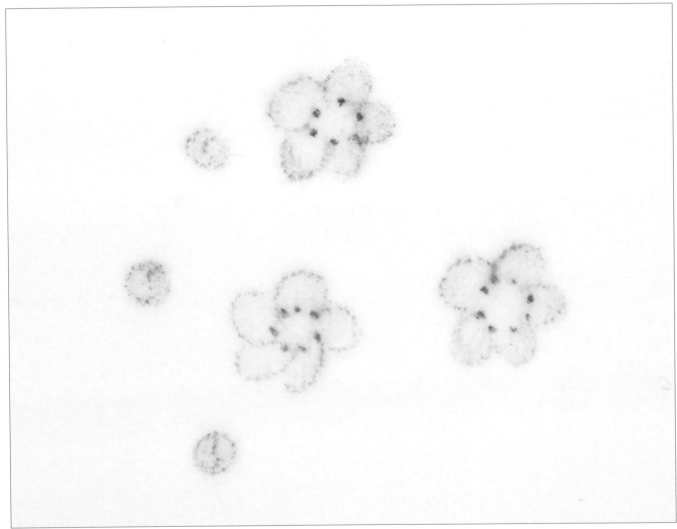

Put a circle of burnt sienna dots in the center of each flower. Leave enough space in the middle of the circle to put in a dot of acrylic yellow after all detail is done.

- **Strawberry seeds**. Mix alizarin crimson with a small amount of burnt umber, then add a little Turpenoid. Randomly dot the strawberries to create seeds.
- **Leaves**. Mix some greenish umber with chromium oxide green on the palette, and add Turpenoid. Paint the veins, stems, and an uneven number of tendrils.

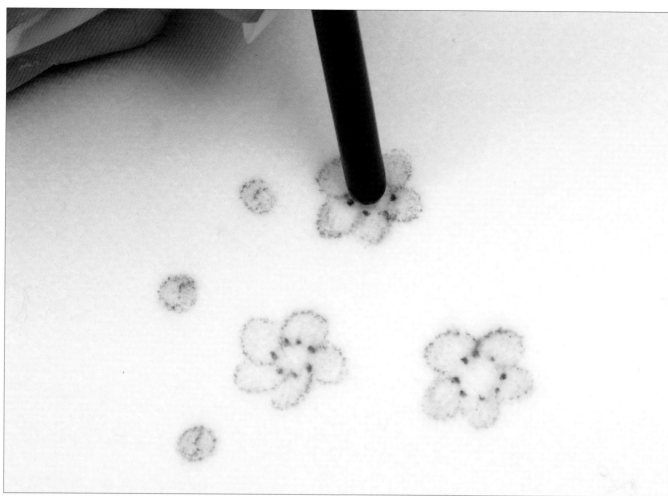

• **Flower centers**. Using the handle end of your liner brush, dip the tip into the cadmium yellow acrylic paint, and gently touch this to the center of each flower.

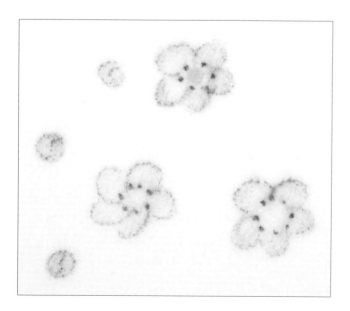

# Bleeding Heart Trinket Box

This project was inspired by the trinket box made in 1834 by Susan Croasdale, who painted the theorem with oils on velvet (see page 14). After the painting dried, she glued it to the top of the red box and covered the edges with gold embossed paper. She then signed her name and the date on the bottom of the box. Once the stencils are cut, painting and finishing the box is quick work. This would make a lovely gift filled with chocolates.

## Palette

- yellow ochre
- burnt sienna
- alizarin crimson golden
- chromium oxide green
- sap green
- greenish umber
- Permalba white

## Additional Supplies

- $3^3/_8$ x $4^1/_2$-inch paper box from a craft store
- embossed paper
- Elmer's Painters gold metallic opaque marker
- gold spray paint
- 3M Spray Mount adhesive
- red or green acrylic paint

### PREPARING THE BOX

Paint the box with two or three coats of a red acrylic paint that will complement the red in the theorem. Alternatively, you could use a green to match the leaves. I had some Benjamin Moore paint number 1309 left over from another project and used it for the base of the box. The stripe was done with a fine-point Elmer's Painters metallic opaque marker. Use a cork-backed ruler to keep the line straight along the lower edge.

### PREPARING THE VELVET AND STENCILS

Trace the pattern for the bleeding heart. Trace and cut the stencils for the painting. Mount the velvet for painting the pincushions following the instructions on page 106. Place strips of the stencil material along the top and

bottom edges of the mounted velvet. Center the first stencil on the velvet and secure in place with masking tape at the top and bottom. Read through the instructions in each stencil section before beginning to paint.

### MIXING COLORS

**Bleeding hearts.** Mix a little burnt sienna with some alizarin crimson golden to create a golden red-brown. Try to come close to the red color you are using as the base paint of your box.

### STENCIL NUMBER 1

- **Bleeding hearts.** Base-paint the bleeding heart flowers with the alizarin crimson golden–burnt sienna mix. Paint the area on the left flower that is behind the front flower a deeper value.
- **Leaf.** Base-paint the leaf with yellow ochre, then shade with chromium oxide green.

### STENCIL NUMBER 2

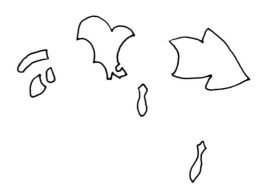

- **Bleeding hearts.** Base-paint the bleeding heart flower with the alizarin crimson golden–burnt sienna mixture. Shade the areas that are behind the front three flowers a deeper value.

- **Teardrops of the flowers and buds**. Base-paint with Permalba white. Shade the edges with a light layer of sap green along the side edges only.
- **Leaf**. Base-paint the leaf with yellow ochre, then shade with chromium oxide green.

## STENCIL NUMBER 3

- **Bleeding hearts and buds**. Base-paint the bleeding heart flower with the alizarin crimson golden–burnt sienna mixture. Paint the buds with the same red mixture. Paint along the lower edge of the bud on the top a deeper value.
- **Leaf**. This leaf is painted with a two-stencil technique, using stencil numbers 3 and 4. Keep the green light. Base-paint the leaf with yellow ochre; then paint a light coat of chromium oxide green.

## STENCIL NUMBER 4

- **Bleeding heart buds**. Base-paint the buds with the alizarin crimson golden–burnt sienna mixture.
- **Leaf**. Paint all along the upper edge of the leaf a darker value of chromium oxide green. Keep the center a light green.

## DETAIL

- **Teardrops**. Mix some Turpenoid with a small amount of the alizarin crimson golden–burnt sienna mixture. Outline the teardrops with a fine line.
- **Leaf veins and stems**. Mix a small amount of greenish umber with some chromium oxide green. Add a touch of sap green to brighten the color slightly. Then add some Turpenoid to make a watery mixture. Paint the veins on the leaves and some fine lines for stems.

## ASSEMBLING THE BOX

Let the painting dry for several days before assembling the box. When completely dry, remove the tape from the velvet, releasing it from the flat surface.

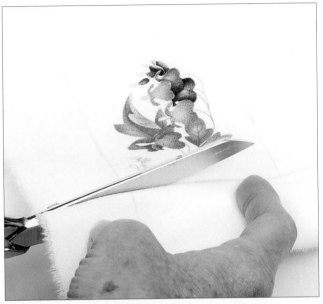

Trim the velvet painting to a 3³⁄₄ x 2³⁄₄-inch rectangle. Turn facedown in a box or on a piece of newspaper.

Apply a spray adhesive liberally to the back of the painting.

Carefully center the painting on the lid of the prepared box, then gently press it securely in place.

If gold embossed paper is not available, purchase white embossed paper and spray with metallic gold paint. Several coats of the spray paint will be needed. Let dry after each coat. Cut the paper into $5/16$-inch-wide strips. Cut two of these strips to a length of $4^1/8$ inches and two shorter strips $3^1/4$ inches long. Lay the strips on the box lid, covering the edge of the velvet to check the fit. Trim the ends of each strip on an angle to create a mitered appearance in each corner.

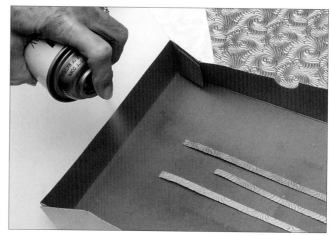

Lay the strips upside down in a box lid or on newspaper and spray the back of the paper strips with the adhesive.

Place one of these longer strips along the edge of the velvet. Press firmly into place.

Then place the other long strip along the opposite edge of the painting. The short side of the strip is closest to the painting. Press firmly into place.

Place one of these short strips along one side of the picture, covering the velvet edge with the shorter side of the strip closest to the painting. Press firmly into place.

Place the other short strip on the remaining side, covering the edge of the velvet. Press firmly into place.

### STRIPE ON BOTTOM OF BOX

Place a 6-inch cork-backed ruler $1/4$ inch from the bottom of the box.

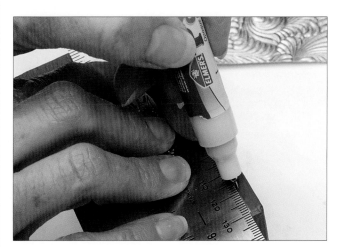

Run the Elmer's Painters gold metallic opaque marker along the ruler to make the stripe.

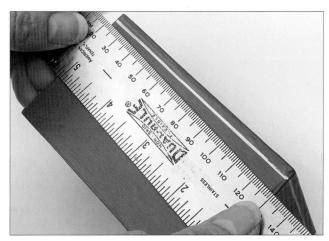

Be sure to line up the ruler at each corner with the previously striped side.

## Mounting Velvet for a Box or Pillow

You may want to use a theorem for a pillow, pincushion, or lid of a box. Cut the velvet $1^1/4$ inch larger on all sides to allow for taping to a hard surface and for subsequent seams.

Cut a piece of velvet $4^1/2$ x $5^3/4$ inches for the theorem. Remove any lint on the back of the velvet. Place the velvet on a smooth hard surface such as the glass for cutting stencils.

Tape the right edge of the velvet to the surface. Press the tape firmly.

Place the tape on the left edge of the velvet. Stretch the velvet taut as you secure it to the surface.

Tape the top of the velvet to the surface.

Place a piece of tape along the lower edge of the velvet. Then, stretch the velvet as you secure it to the surface.

# American Copper Butterfly

The American copper butterfly in this theorem is enhanced with nontoxic powders, which add a visual dimension that can fool the eye and give the painting a more realistic look. It is also lovely without the powders. This design does not need to be enlarged; it will fit a 6 x 8-inch frame. The leaves are painted using two stencils.

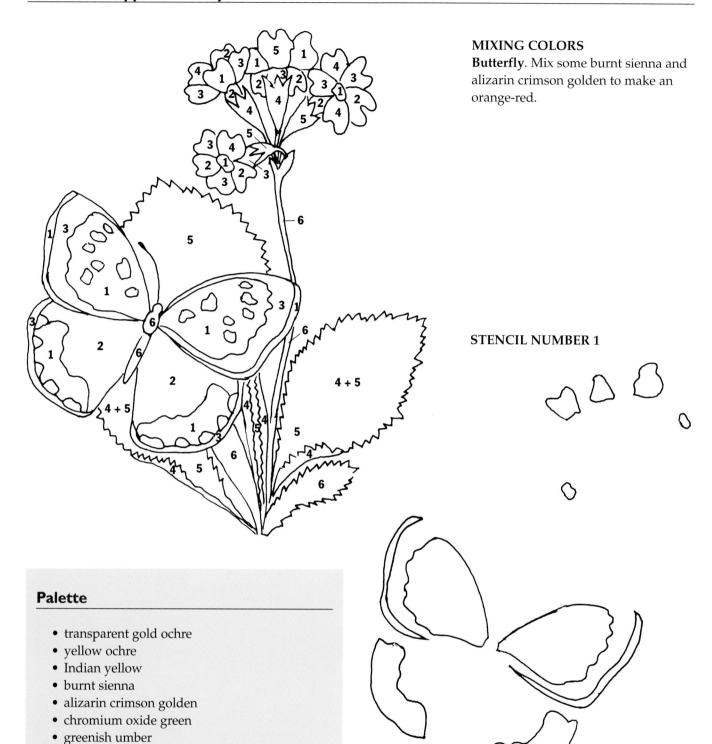

**MIXING COLORS**

**Butterfly**. Mix some burnt sienna and alizarin crimson golden to make an orange-red.

**STENCIL NUMBER 1**

## Palette

- transparent gold ochre
- yellow ochre
- Indian yellow
- burnt sienna
- alizarin crimson golden
- chromium oxide green
- greenish umber
- burnt umber

## Additional Supplies

- Pearl Ex, nontoxic powdered pigments by Jacquard
- small flat brush
- small round liner brush

- **Primula**. Base-paint the primula petals with Indian yellow, then shade along the edges with transparent gold ochre.
- **Butterfly**. Paint a thin edge of Davy's gray on the outside edge of the top two butterfly wings.

  Paint the rest of the wings with the alizarin crimson golden–burnt sienna mix.

**STENCIL NUMBER 2**

- **Primulas**. Base-paint the primula petals with Indian yellow, then shade the edges with transparent gold ochre. Deepen areas that are behind another petal.
- **Butterfly**. Base-paint the wings with a light shading of burnt umber. Place a curved shield over the light burnt umber and shade along the edge a darker value of burnt umber. Use the dotted lines on the drawing as a suggestion for placement.

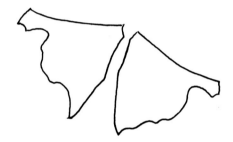

**STENCIL NUMBER 3**

- **Primula**. Base-paint the primula petals with Indian yellow, then shade the edges with transparent gold ochre. Deepen areas that are behind another petal.
- **Butterfly**. Paint a thin strip of Davy's gray on the outside edges of the lower butterfly wings. Paint the top wings with burnt umber.
- **Leaf**. Base paint with yellow ochre. Shade with chromium oxide of green. Add a little Prussian blue to the right side, blending into the green.

**STENCIL NUMBER 4**

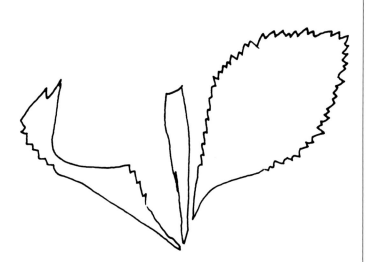

**STENCIL NUMBER 5**

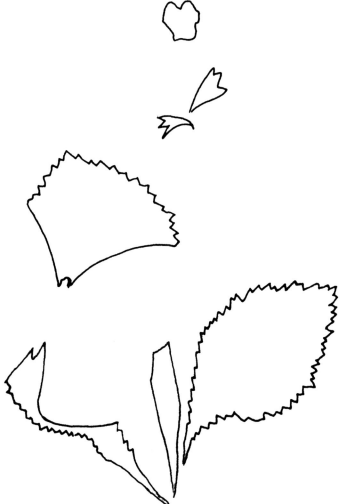

- **Leaf**. Base-paint the leaf with yellow ochre, then shade with a very light coat of chromium oxide green.
- **Primulas**. Base-paint the primula petals with Indian yellow, keeping the centers light. Shade the edges with transparent gold ochre.
- **Primula calyx**. Base-paint the calyx with yellow ochre. Shade with chromium oxide green.

- **Primula**. Base-paint the primula petal with Indian yellow, keeping the center light. Shade the edge with transparent gold ochre.
- **Leaves**. Base-paint the leaves with yellow ochre. Shade with chromium oxide green. Shade the lower left and right leaves with Prussian blue, blending into the green.
- **Calyx of the primula**. Base-paint the calyx with yellow ochre. Shade with chromium oxide green.

**STENCIL NUMBER 6**

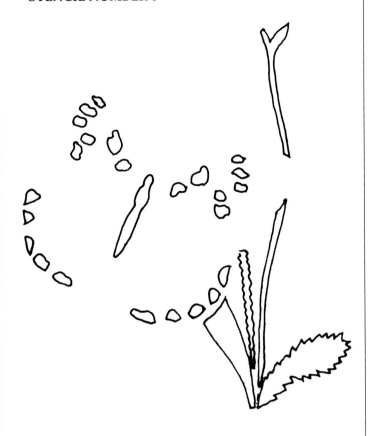

- **Butterfly**. Paint all butterfly markings with burnt umber, making them on the dark side. Paint along the edges of the body with burnt umber, keeping the center light.
- **Primula stem and leaves**. Base-paint the stems and leaves with yellow ochre. Shade with chromium oxide green. Add some Prussian blue to the leaves.

**DETAIL**

- **Primulas**. Add some Turpenoid to the alizarin crimson–burnt sienna mixture. Paint three little dots in the center of the right and lower primula.
- **Leaf veins**. Mix a little Prussian blue with some chromium oxide green, then add some Turpenoid. Paint some wiggly lines to represent the veins.
- **Butterfly**. Mix some Turpenoid and burnt umber. Paint the antennae on the butterfly with some of this mixture.

**IRIDESCENT POWDERS ON THE WINGS**

Cut a 6 x 8-inch piece of tracing paper. Trace the butterfly onto the tracing paper. Then cut out the butterfly. Place this over the painted butterfly. This template will prevent the powders from getting onto the velvet where you don't want them. These nontoxic powders float in the air and also can scatter if the nap of the velvet catches the tip of the brush.

Dip a liner brush into the white iridescent powder.

Carefully paint the white powder onto the white edges of the butterfly wings. Wipe the powder from the brush.

Dip a small, flat brush into the iridescent copper powder. Gently lay the iridescent copper powder on the red wing areas, painting with the grain of the fabric.

Dip the same brush into the iridescent brown powder. Lay some of the iridescent brown powder on the dark brown area of each wing with the small, flat brush. Then, with the liner brush, paint the brown spots on the wings with the iridescent brown powder.

Carefully remove the tracing-paper template.

Wipe the iridescent copper powder out of the brush.

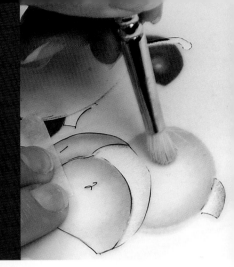

# Canton Bowl of Cherries and Apricots

This design was created from some of my still-life compositions and photographs. I based the bowl on pieces of antique blue and white pottery I've seen over the years. If cherries are not in season, refer to a catalog that sells fruit trees for accurate colors. You can vary the design by substituting yellow cherries for red and peaches instead of apricots. The design does not need to be enlarged to fit beautifully in an 8 x 10-inch frame. You will learn some new techniques in painting this theorem, so read through the entire stenciling portion before beginning to paint. For stencils, see pages 25 and 28 to 33.

## Palette

- transparent gold ochre
- yellow ochre
- Indian yellow
- alizarin crimson
- alizarin crimson golden
- Grumbacher red
- chromium oxide green
- Prussian blue
- raw umber
- Permalba white

### MIXING COLORS

- **Apricots.** To make a soft yellow for the apricots, put a generous quarter-size dollop of Permalba white on your palette. Add a small amount of the following colors in the order presented, mixing well after each addition: yellow ochre, Indian yellow, and transparent gold ochre. Then divide your mixture into three portions. Leave one as is. To the second, add a touch of Grumbacher red and raw umber, making a peachy yellow. To the third, add a bit more Grumbacher red along with a touch of alizarin crimson golden to create the third color for the apricots. Transfer these colors to your main palette in order from light to dark under the yellows in the Perfect Palette lineup.
- **Cherries.** Mix alizarin crimson with a small amount of Prussian blue on the palette. Be careful not to make purple. Place this color mix under the reds on your main painting palette.
- **Canton bowl.** Mix Prussian blue with some raw umber to create a deep greenish blue. Place this color under the blue section on your main palette.

### STENCIL NUMBER 1

- **Canton bowl.** With the Prussian blue–raw umber mixture, paint along the edges of the bowl with soft strokes going from one side to the other, very lightly fading to white in the middle. The bowl should be a very pale shade of the blue.

At this time, replace the saved bowl stencil piece in its opening to protect the painted bowl. Proceed with the rest of the stencil.

- **Apricot.** Base-paint the complete apricot with the lightest color value. Place a curve at the point of the apricot. Then shade the edges of this curve with the medium color mixture, and pull some of this color in toward the center of the apricot. Add the third color along the edges of the top and bottom of the apricot. Lightly shade the top with a little raw umber to create depth in the fruit. "Less is best" when it comes to shading the apricots with the raw umber. Remove the curve.
- **Cherries.** On the cherry with an exposed stem area, use Indian yellow to lightly paint the area for the dot that is marked on your drawing.

## Tips

- Trace the apricot curve on a small piece of stencil film. Cut this curve to use when painting the apricots.
- Trace the dotted lines on the "save" apricot on stencil number 2. When it is cut from the stencil, number the sections and cut apart.
- Cut small curves for the cherries.
- Cut a number of tiny oval dots out of masking tape for the cherries.
- For ease in painting, saved stencil pieces can be held in place with small strips of masking tape.
- You will need two or three sheets of palette paper for mixing the paints for this design.

Using the point of an X-acto knife, place one of the masking-tape dots over the yellow paint on the cherry. Make sure the dot is off-center in the area painted yellow.

Now paint the remaining cherries in Grumbacher red, keeping this color ⅛ inch away from the masking tape so that some yellow shows. Over top of the Grumbacher red, paint with alizarin crimson golden. Shade the outside edges of the cherries with the alizarin crimson–Prussian blue mixture. Place the curve on each cherry, and deepen along the curve.

With a number 1 stencil brush, paint a darker curved line in a circle with the alizarin crimson–Prussian blue mixture ⅛ inch from the yellow area on top of the Grumbacher red–alizarin crimson golden base. Leave some of the base color showing between the yellow and the dark red mixture.

**STENCIL NUMBER 2**
• **Apricot**. Base-paint both apricots in the lightest value.

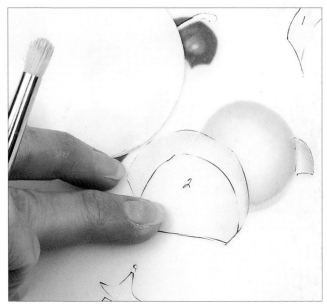

Place the two saved pieces of apricot stencil numbers 2 and 3 back in the opening of the center apricot. In the dip created by the two replaced pieces, lightly shade the area with raw umber. Shade the top of the fruit with the two other apricot colors, starting with the medium value.

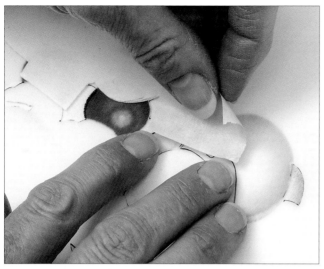

Remove the piece from stencil number 2, and place the section from stencil number 1 over the area that you just painted. Shade the exposed area with the two apricot colors, starting with the medium value first, then the darker one. Enhance the apricot cheek with lightly applied alizarin crimson golden.

Remove the number 3 piece, and replace number 2. Keep section number 1 in position. Shade the right side with the middle value first and the deepest value last. Add more alizarin crimson golden as desired.

- **Triangular apricot.** Shade the outer edge of the apricot with the middle value, then shade the outer edge with the third.
- **Cherry stems.** Base-paint a light wash of Indian yellow. Use a small curved shield to cover the ends of the stems away from the fruit. They need to be kept lighter than the rest of the stems. Shade the stems lightly with chromium oxide green.
- **Cherries.** Base-paint the cherries with Grumbacher red, then shade with alizarin crimson golden. Finally, using the alizarin crimson–Prussian blue mixture, deepen any areas of the cherries that are behind another cherry.
- **Scene on bowl.** Use the Prussian blue–raw umber mixture to paint the boat and its roofs. Then paint along the edges of the roofs of the big house, leaving the centers light. Use the same mixture for the bird on the left side of the bowl and the roof on the lower left of the bowl. Deepen the right side of the roof. Next, paint the ground around the house, deepening the areas that are behind the hill on the right and under the tree on the left. Paint the hill on the right side of the bowl, using a darker value on the left side of the opening. Finally, paint the ground on the bottom of the bowl.

**STENCIL NUMBER 3**
- **Canton bowl.** With the Prussian blue–raw umber mixture, paint the tree, keeping the bottom of the trunk a lighter color. Paint along the edges of the house in the middle of the bowl, keeping the center light. Then paint the front of the house on the lower left side of the bowl, again keeping the center light. Finally, paint the hill on the right.
- **Cherries.** On the cherry next to the apricots, using Indian yellow, lightly paint the area to the left of center that is marked on your drawing. Place a masking-tape dot on the cherry using the point of an X-acto knife, as in the photo. Paint this cherry and all the remaining cherries with Grumbacher red, then alizarin crimson golden. Place a curve on each cherry and shade with the alizarin crimson–Prussian blue mixture. Deepen any areas that are behind another cherry.
- **Apricots.** Base-paint both apricots with the lightest of the apricot colors. Place a curve on the fruit, lining it up with the point on the left side. Shade the upper side of the apricot that is exposed with the medium color, then paint the deepest color along the curve.

Add a small amount of alizarin crimson golden to enhance the apricot. On the right apricot, shade the upper edge first with the medium color, then with the darker color.
- **Apricot stems**. Paint the stems with yellow ochre.

**STENCIL NUMBER 4**
- **Cherries**. On the three lower left cherries, paint some Indian yellow on the area where they are joined to the stem. Place a shield over each area to be left for the stems. Paint all the cherries with Grumbacher red, leaving $1/8$ inch of yellow showing near the stem joint, then overpaint the red with alizarin crimson golden. Shade the cherries with the alizarin crimson–Prussian blue mixture $1/8$ inch from the area you just painted, using a shield to create a crease.
- **Left apricot**. Base-paint the apricot with the lightest color first, then apply the medium value on the outer edges. Shade in the perimeter with raw umber to create the illusion that this apricot is behind the other fruit.
- **Right apricot**. Base-paint with the lightest color. Position a curve off-center on the right side of the apricot. Shade the exposed area with the medium value, followed by the deepest color along the edge. On the left side of the fruit, use raw umber to make this apricot appear to be behind the others. Remove the curve, and shade along the edge of the right side with the medium apricot color.
- **Apricot stems**. Shade the outer edges of the stems with raw umber. Where a stem extends into the curved painted area of the apricot, place a shield over the exposed portion before painting so that the stem will sit correctly on the fruit.
- **Canton bowl**. With the Prussian blue–raw umber mixture, paint the leaves on the tree and along the edges of the bridge. Then paint the side of the house on the lower left of the bowl.

**STENCIL NUMBER 5**
- **Cherries**. Paint the stem joint areas of the cherries with Indian yellow. Place an oval dot slightly off-center on each cherry using an X-acto knife. Then paint all the cherries with Grumbacher red, overpaint with alizarin crimson golden, and shade with the alizarin crimson–Prussian blue mixture.

- **Canton bowl**. Shade the sides and bottom of the foot of the bowl with the Prussian blue–raw umber mixture. Paint the band on the bowl a deeper value of the same color.

   Remove the stencil and masking-tape dots, and continue with the detail work.

**DETAIL**
- **Cherry stems**. Add Turpenoid to the chromium oxide green paint, and paint a circle around the end of each cherry stem.
- **Cherries**. Using a liner brush, paint a thin circle of the same mixture in the center of the yellow area on each cherry.
- **Apricot stems**. Add some Turpenoid to the raw umber, and paint a circle around the top of the apricot stems.

## Design Notes for Stencils

**STENCIL NUMBER 1**
- Trace and cut the entire bowl shape minus the foot.

**STENCIL NUMBER 2**
- Trace and cut the hill on the right of the boat. Do not cut the tree, which will be painted using linework.
- Trace and cut the roofs of the houses on the boat.
- Trace and cut the large apricot, saving the cutout piece. Then trace the curved lines and number the sections. Cut apart.
- Trace and cut all cherry stems.

**STENCIL NUMBER 3**
- Trace and cut the entire apricot stem. The lower part will be painted with stencil 4.

**STENCIL NUMBER 4**
- Trace and cut the small triangle between the two large apricots along the rim of the bowl.
- Trace and cut the bridge.
- Trace and cut the stem portion of the apricot indicated on your drawing.

- **Lines on Canton bowl**. Add Turpenoid and a drop of Skin So Soft to the Prussian blue–raw umber mixture. Carefully paint a fine line around the outer edge of the bowl and another along the upper edge. Paint a third line $1/8$ inch from and parallel to the blue band. Then paint a fine line around the foot.
- **Details on bowl**. Paint the following details on the Canton bowl with the same mixture. Begin with the tree on the right side of the bowl. Then paint lines on the boat to complete the house and for the mast and support ropes. Also on the boat, paint the figure of a man with a pole. On the large house, paint the roof support poles, squares for the windows, and the door frame. Make some zigzag lines on the bridge. Outline the front of the house on the left. Create roof tiles by painting horizontal lines and then vertical lines to connect them. Define the bird on the left by outlining it. Between the large tree and the main house, paint two more birds each with two curved lines. Finish by painting some wiggly lines for water behind the island, around the boat, and between the house and bridge.

# Mallard Duck

My son and son-in-law love the outdoors and all aspects of nature. Both enjoy fishing, and my son likes to hunt as well. I designed the Mallard Duck theorem with all lovers of nature in mind. This project explores shading techniques in detail. Enlarge the design 105 percent to fit a 9 x 12-inch frame.

## Palette

- transparent gold ochre
- yellow ochre
- Indian yellow
- burnt sienna
- alizarin crimson
- Grumbacher red
- chromium oxide green
- sap green
- Prussian blue
- burnt umber
- raw umber
- Permalba white
- Turpenoid

### MIXING COLORS

- **Teal blue feathers**. Mix Prussian blue with a small amount of raw umber to create a deep teal blue.
- **Mallard's breast**. Mix Grumbacher red with burnt sienna. Then add a small amount of alizarin crimson and a touch of burnt umber to make a reddish orange-brown.

### STENCIL NUMBER 1

- **Wing**. Cut the saved wing along the dotted line indicated on the pattern.

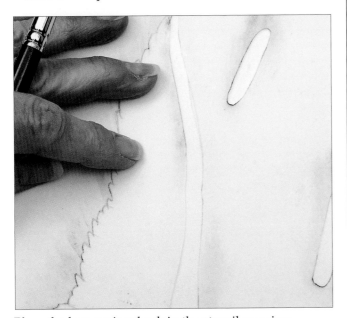

Place the larger piece back in the stencil opening.

Pick up a very small amount of burnt umber on the stencil brush.

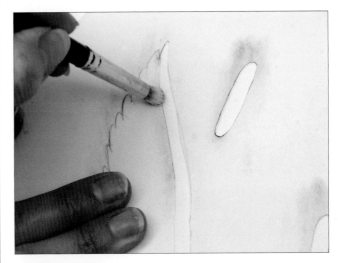

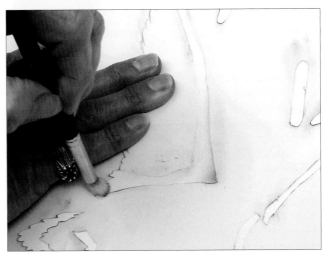

Shade both sides of the opening between the wing edge and the replaced stencil piece. Do not apply this brown too heavily, or the detail will not be apparent later.

**Stencil Number 1**

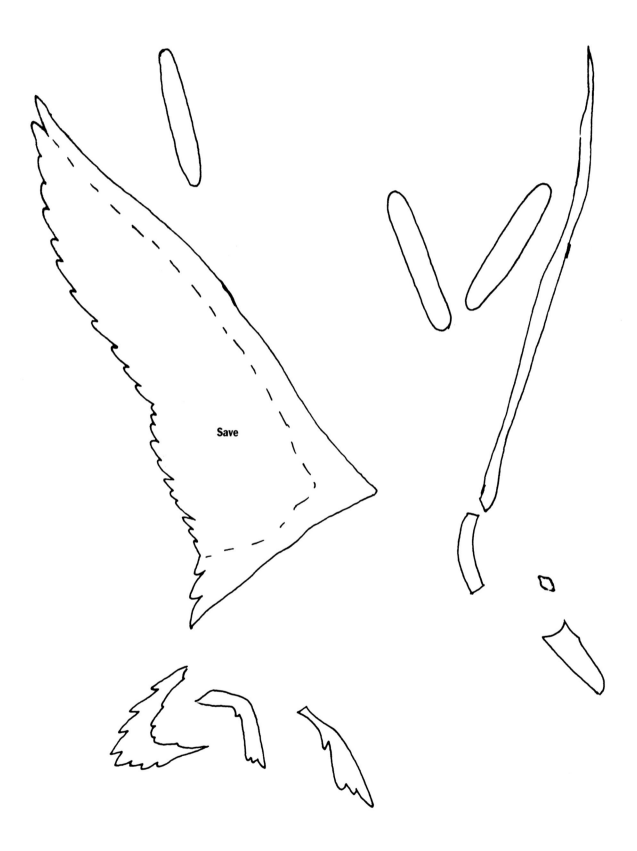

Save

Remove the wing piece.

Reposition the wing cutout, lining up the point in the wing stencil with the shield to define the first of two long wing feathers. Shade along the edge of the shield with burnt umber, painting only about three inches down the cutout. Move the cutout and position it parallel to the first feather. Shade along the cutout about 3 inches. Remove this wing piece and set aside.

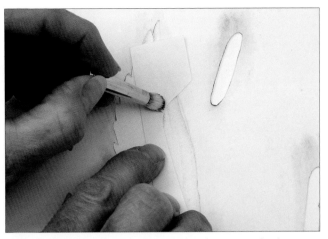

Place a shield with a shallow curve between the bases of the two long feathers, and shade with burnt umber along the shallow curve about 2 inches, creating the first of five feathers.

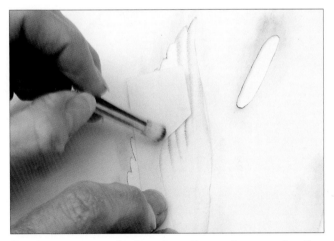

Continue to create feathers in a diagonal row under the first one you painted, until you have five of these feathers in the row.

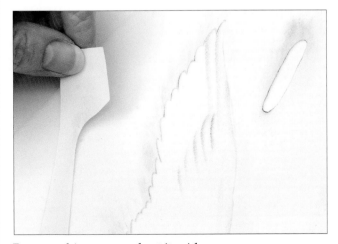

Remove this curve and set it aside.

Line up the saved wing piece with the points on the wing stencil, and shade some feathers along the edge of the wing piece to the inner wing feathers.

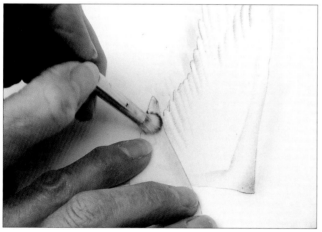

Continue shading in feathers down the side until you are close to the shading of the wing that you originally painted in.

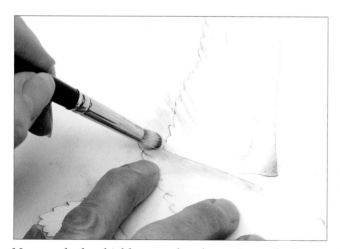

Now angle the shield upward and, starting at the bottom of the wing, shade in three different feathers.

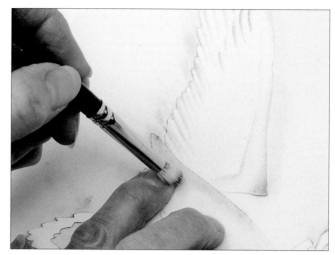

Then shade in the feathers that are not completed on the wing, following the angle of the ones above.

This is how the completed stenciled feather will look.

- **Neck**. Paint the neck with Permalba white.
- **Bill and feet**. Base-paint the bill and feet with Indian yellow, and shade with transparent gold ochre. Use a shield to define the toes and upper and lower bills.
- **Eye**. Paint the eye with the same two colors.
- **Tail**. Starting at the body end, paint the tail with the Prussian blue–raw umber mixture, and then switch to plain raw umber for the tips of the tail feathers. Keep the raw umber light so the detail work will show up later.
- **Cattails**. Base-paint the cattails with yellow ochre, then shade with burnt sienna, leaving the centers a lighter brown. Finally, apply burnt umber to the edges.
- **Leaf**. Base-paint the leaf with yellow ochre, then shade with chromium oxide green.

**Stencil Number 2**

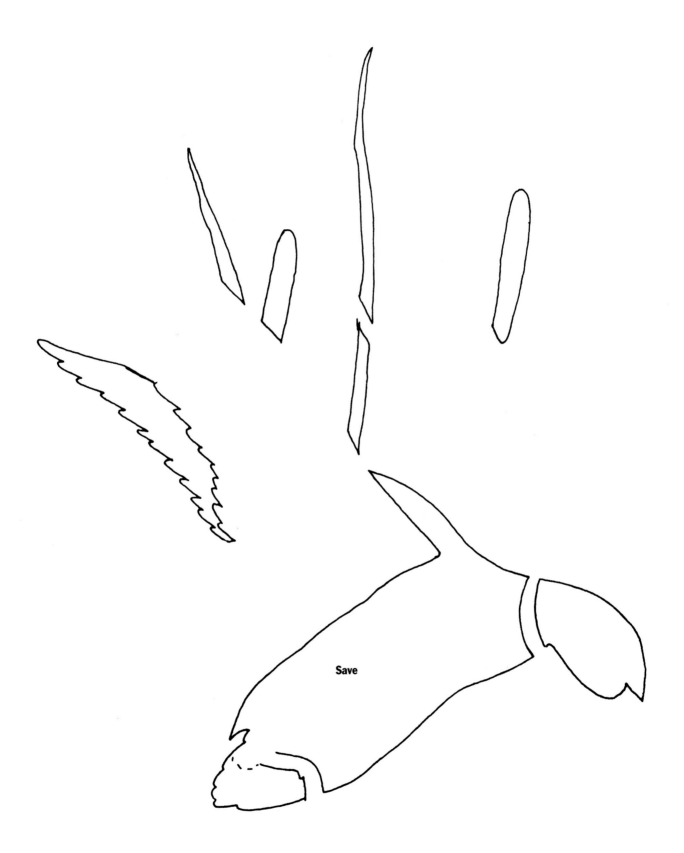

Save

**Stencil Number 3**

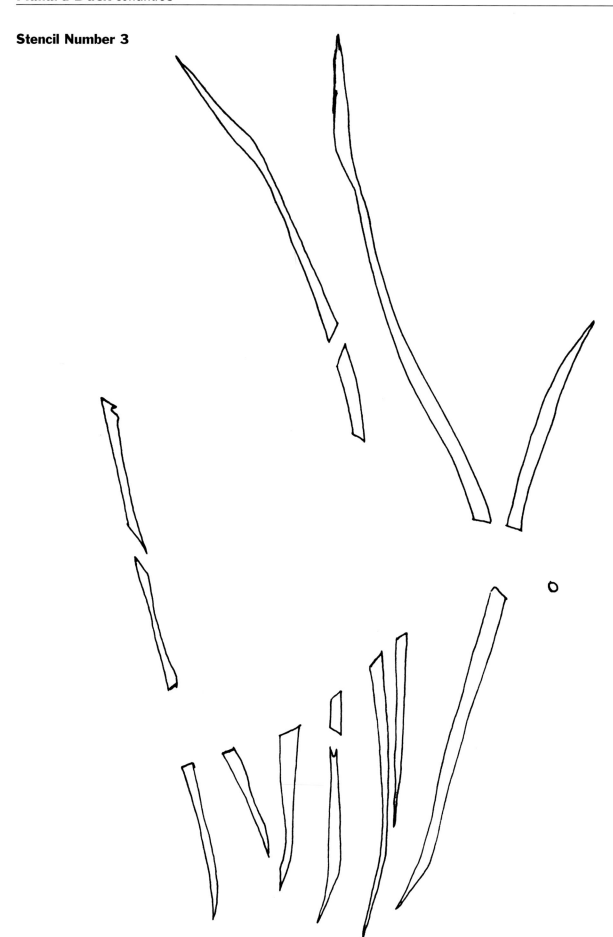

**Stencil Number 4**

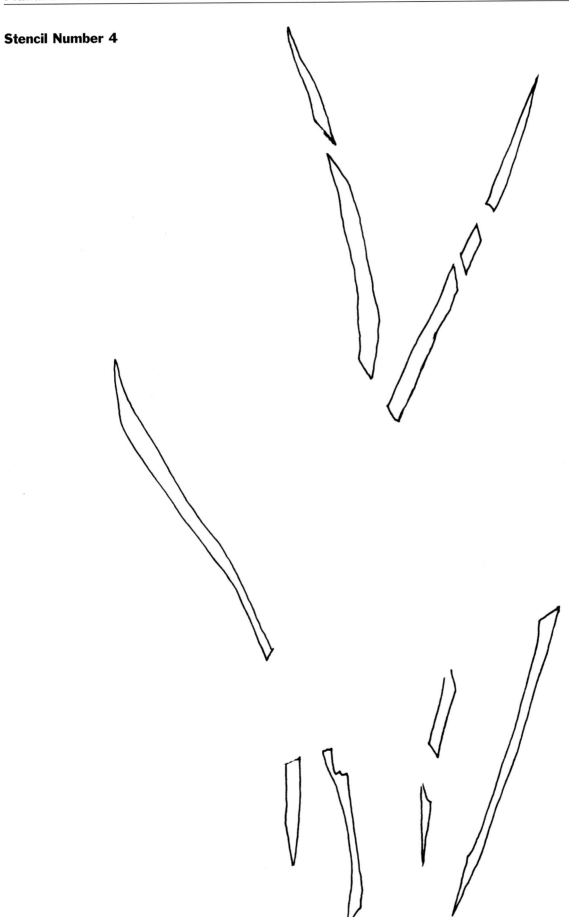

**STENCIL NUMBER 2**

- **Body**. Cut the saved body piece along the dotted line. Place the bottom section in place, and shade the mallard along the lower edge of the body, leg, and wing with a light value of burnt umber. Shade the neck area with the red breast color mixture, fading out into the body. Paint the shoulder a light value of the teal blue mixture.
- **Wing**. Mix equal amounts of burnt umber and raw umber, and shade the area on the wing that is behind the first wing with this mixture. Using a shield, shade the feathers with burnt umber, changing to the teal blue mixture about one-third of the way down the wing.
- **Cattails**. Base-paint the cattails with yellow ochre, then shade with burnt sienna, keeping the center a lighter brown. Shade the edges with burnt umber.
- **Leaves**. Base-paint the leaves with yellow ochre, and shade with chromium oxide green.
- **Head**. Cut a masking-tape oval to cover the yellow-painted eye area, and place over the eye with the tip of an X-acto knife. Base-paint the head with sap green, followed by the teal blue mixture along the edges. Give contour to the head by deepening the cheek and rear eye area with the teal blue.

**STENCIL NUMBER 3**

- **Eye**. Paint the eye with burnt umber.
- **Leaves**. Base-paint the leaves with yellow ochre, then shade with chromium oxide green.

**STENCIL NUMBER 4**

- **Leaves**. Paint the leaves the same way as with stencil 3.

**DETAIL**

Mix Turpenoid with burnt umber, and define each feather with quick, little strokes. Add a curl at the end of each tail feather. Outline the eye, and add a few brush strokes on the face. Paint two little marks on the bill to indicate the nostrils. Use the same mixture for the stems of the cattails. Mix some chromium oxide green with the burnt umber, and paint the center veins in the leaves.

# Vase of Flowers

The soft hues in this serene vase of flowers are difficult to achieve, especially for those of us who like rich colors and enjoy expressing ourselves with them. Enlarge the drawing 125 percent. This will fit an 11 x 14-inch frame. Mix all the colors with Liquin as indicated below before you begin to paint. Use the Liquin with caution; review the instructions on Mixing Liquin and Paints found on page 17.

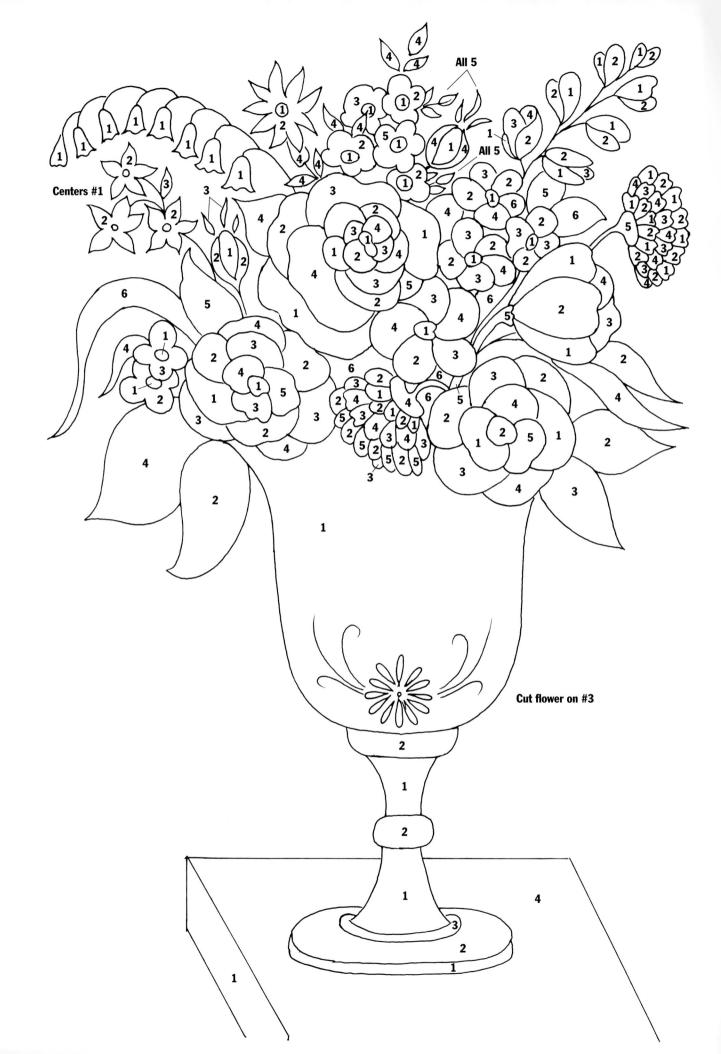

## Palette

- transparent gold ochre
- yellow ochre
- Indian yellow
- burnt sienna
- alizarin crimson
- alizarin crimson golden
- chromium oxide green
- greenish umber
- Prussian blue
- raw umber
- Davy's gray
- Payne's gray
- Liquin
- Turpenoid

### MIXING COLORS

- **Alabaster**. Mix some Liquin with Prussian blue to make a soft blue. Add some Liquin to a small amount of alizarin crimson for a soft red-pink.
- **Vase**. Add some Liquin to a bit of Payne's gray to create a pale gray.
- **Left and center roses and buds**. Mix some Liquin with alizarin crimson to make a soft red.
- **Bluebells and delphinium buds**. Mix Liquin with some Prussian blue to create a soft blue that is a shade darker than the alabaster color.
- **Pink rose on right**. Mix some Liquin with alizarin crimson golden to make a lovely pink.

## Design Notes for Stencils

- Cut the centers of the blue star flowers on the right on stencil number 1. Cut the flower in the bowl of the vase on stencil number 3.

## Tips on Painting the Center Rose

- When painting the center rose in the Vase of Flowers design, keep in mind that Davy's gray always shows darker than you expect once the stencil is removed. Practice the following steps for creating this rose on a small piece of velvet before painting it on your theorem. Use plenty of shields.

### STENCIL NUMBER 1

- **Vase**. With a large brush, gently shade the vase along all the edges with the Payne's gray–Liquin mixture, fading out to the velvet color. Make the color slightly darker along the lower curve of the vase.
- **Vase stem**. Shade along the edges of these two pieces with the Payne's gray–Liquin mixture, making the bottom of each section a little darker.
- **Side of alabaster base**. Paint the edge of the alabaster base with a very light value of raw umber. With a small brush, paint some of the Prussian blue mixed with Liquin here and there on the side of the base. Shade the base side the same way as was done with the blue, using the alizarin crimson–Liquin mixture.
- **Bluebells and delphinium buds**. Base-paint the petals of both the bluebells and the delphiniums with the Prussian blue–Liquin mixture, making the edges darker than the centers.
- **Bluet flower centers**. Base-paint the bluet flower centers Indian yellow.
- **Centers of white daisy, white and variegated primroses, and buttercup**. Base-paint these flower centers with Indian yellow, then shade their lower portions with transparent gold ochre.
- **Yellow crocus**. Base-paint the crocus petals with Indian yellow, keeping the centers light. Deepen the curve toward the center of each petal with transparent gold ochre.
- **Center rose**.

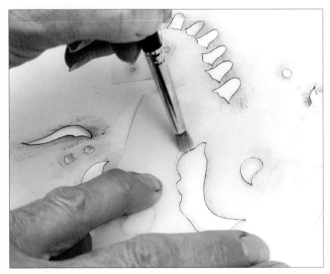

Paint the outer edge with the alizarin crimson–Liquin mixture, fading quickly to the color of the velvet.

**Stencil Number 2**

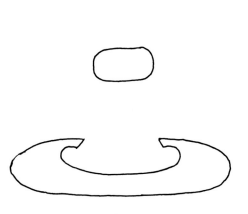

Paint each petal on the area toward the center of the flower with Davy's gray. Use very little paint, and fade quickly to the velvet color.

Here is what the flower petals should look like when stencil 1 is completed.

- **Rosebuds**. Paint along the edges of the buds, keeping the centers white.
- **Red rose on left**. Base-paint the petals a pale red with the alizarin crimson–Liquin mixture. Deepen the color on the part of each petal facing the center of the flower.
- **Pink rose on right**. Base-paint the petals a pale pink with the alizarin crimson golden–Liquin mixture. Darken the part of each petal that faces the center of the flower.
- **Chrysanthemums**. Use pure Prussian blue to paint the chrysanthemums starting at the base of each petal and fading quickly to a light blue.

**STENCIL NUMBER 2**
- **Vase**. Shade along the edges of the vase stem sections with the Payne's gray–Liquin mixture, fading out to the color of the velvet. On the foot of the vase, shade along the lower outer edges only.
- **White primroses**. Paint the edges of the primroses with Davy's gray, fading to the color of the velvet.

- **Daisy**. Working on one petal at a time, place a curved shield on the point closest to the center of the flower. Shade the edge of this curve with Davy's gray, fading out near the yellow center. Reposition the curve for each petal.
- **Delphinium buds**. Paint the delphinium buds with a light coat of the Prussian blue–Liquin mixture. On each petal, deepen the edge that faces the center of the flower.
- **Bluets**. Paint the flowers with Prussian blue, fading to white toward the center.
- **Chrysanthemums**. Use pure Prussian blue to paint the petals, starting at the base of each and fading quickly to a light blue at the tips.
- **Crocus**. Base-paint the petal with Indian yellow, then enhance with a streak or two of transparent gold ochre to define the petal.
- **Buttercup**. Base-paint the petal with Indian yellow, then shade from the top right and halfway around the lower portion of the petal with transparent gold ochre.
- **Center rose**.

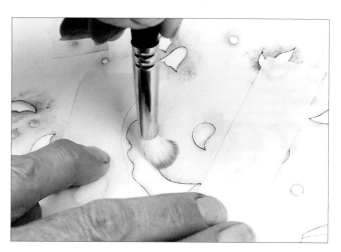

Paint each petal on the area toward the center of the flower with Davy's gray. Again use very little paint and fade quickly to the color of the velvet.

**Stencil Number 3**

**Stencil Number 4**

Paint the outer edge with the alizarin crimson–Liquin mixture, fading quickly to the velvet color.

- **Red rose on left**. Base-paint the petals a pale red with the alizarin crimson–Liquin mixture. Deepen the color on the part of each petal that faces the center of the flower.
- **Pink rose on right**. Base-paint the petals a pale pink using the alizarin crimson golden–Liquin mixture. Darken the part of each petal facing the center of the flower.
- **Leaves and calyx**. Base-paint the leaves and calyx with yellow ochre. On the lower right leaf, add some burnt sienna to the upper edge. Then shade all leaves with chromium oxide green.
- **Variegated primroses**. Paint each petal with both alizarin crimson and Prussian blue, fading the colors into each other. Be careful not to blend the colors and make a purple hue. Vary the placement of the colors on each primrose. Deepen the concave parts of the petals to create the appearance that one petal is behind another.

## STENCIL NUMBER 3
- **Flower on vase and foot of vase**. Paint the flower with the Payne's gray–Liquin mixture, and darken the outer and inner edges. Shade the foot of the vase along the lower edge only.
- **White primrose**. Paint the edge of this flower with Davy's gray.

- **Center rose**.

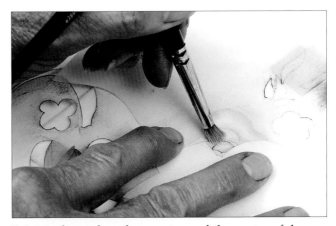

Paint each petal on the area toward the center of the flower with Davy's gray. As before, use very little paint and fade quickly to the color of the velvet.

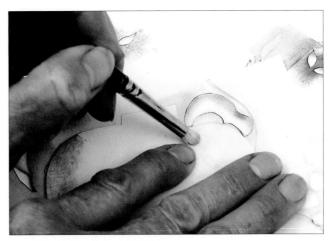

Paint the outer edge with the alizarin crimson–Liquin mix, fading quickly to the velvet color.

Here is what the rose should look like after the first three stencils.

**Stencil Number 5**

**Stencil Number 6**

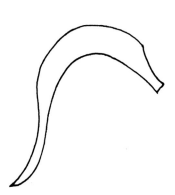

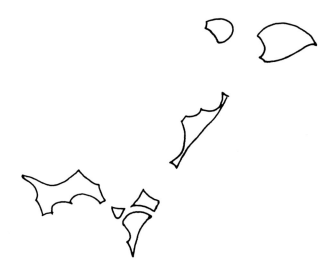

- **Red rose on left**. Base-paint the petals a pale red with the alizarin crimson–Liquin mixture. Deepen the color on the portion of each petal that faces the center of the flower.
- **Pink rose on right**. Base-paint the petals a pale pink using the alizarin crimson golden–Liquin mixture. Darken the part of each petal facing the flower center.
- **Variegated primroses**. Paint both Prussian blue and alizarin crimson on the petals, taking care not to blend the colors into a purple. Vary the placement of the two colors for interest.

- **Crocus and buttercup**. Base-paint the petals with Indian yellow. Use transparent gold ochre to deepen the areas of the crocus petals facing the center of the flower and the concave parts of the buttercup petals.
- **Chrysanthemums**. With pure Prussian blue, paint the petals starting at the base of each and fade quickly to a light blue at the tips.
- **Leaves**. Base-paint the leaves with yellow ochre, then shade with chromium oxide green.

**STENCIL NUMBER 4**

- **Delphinium buds**. Paint the buds a pale blue with a light coat of the Prussian blue–Liquin mixture. Shade along the concave edge of each bud with a darker value of the same blue.
- **Center rose**.

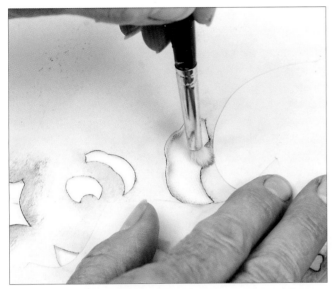

Paint each petal on the area toward the center of the flower with Davy's gray. Use very little paint and fade quickly to the color of the velvet.

Paint the outer edge with the alizarin crimson–Liquin mix, fading quickly to the color of the velvet.

Here is what the center rose looks like after all the stencils have been completed.

- **Red rose on left**. Base-paint the petals a pale red with the alizarin crimson–Liquin mixture. Deepen the color on the part of each petal facing the center of the flower.
- **Pink rose on right**. Base-paint the petals a pale pink with the alizarin crimson golden–Liquin mixture. Darken the portion of each petal that faces the flower center.
- **Crocus and buttercup**. Base-paint the petals of these flowers with Indian yellow. Shade the left side of the crocus petal with transparent gold ochre. On the buttercup, shade with transparent gold ochre the area of the petal that is behind another petal.
- **Chrysanthemums**. Use pure Prussian blue to paint the petals, starting at the base of each and fading quickly to a light blue at the tips.
- **Variegated primroses**. Paint the petals with both alizarin crimson and Prussian blue, taking care not to blend into a purple. Vary the color placement on the petals as before.
- **Leaves and chrysanthemum stem**. Base-paint the leaves and stem with yellow ochre. On the left leaf, add some burnt sienna along the upper edge. Shade the leaves and stem with chromium oxide green.
- **Alabaster base**. Paint the upper edge and right side of the base lightly with raw umber. Using the light Prussian blue and alizarin crimson Liquin mixtures, add streaks of color here and there.

## STENCIL NUMBER 5

- **Center rose**. Paint the petal on the area toward the center of the flower with Davy's gray. Use very little paint, and fade quickly to the color of the velvet. Paint the outer edge of the petal with the alizarin crimson–Liquin mixture, fading quickly to the color of the velvet.
- **Red rose on left**. Base-paint the petal a pale red with the alizarin crimson–Liquin mixture. Deepen the color on the part of the petal that faces the center of the flower.
- **Pink rose on right**. Base-paint the petals a pale pink using the alizarin crimson golden–Liquin mixture. Darken the part of each petal facing the flower center.
- **Chrysanthemums**. Use Prussian pure blue to paint the petals. Start at the base of each and fade quickly to a light blue at the tips.
- **Leaves and stems**. Base-paint the leaves and stems with yellow ochre, then shade with chromium oxide green.

## STENCIL NUMBER 6

- **Variegated primroses**. Paint the petals with both alizarin crimson and Prussian blue, being careful not to blend. Vary the color placement as before.
- **Leaves and background between flowers**. Base-paint the leaves and background areas with yellow ochre; then shade with chromium oxide green. The background in the center should be darker than the stems painted on the earlier stencils.

## DETAIL

- **Buttercup**. Use transparent gold ochre mixed with some Turpenoid to paint a five-petal flower in the center of the buttercup. Dot the area around this with the same mixture.
- **White primroses and daisy**. With the thinned transparent gold ochre, define the bottoms of the flower centers, then add random dots around the yellow center. Place some more dots of burnt sienna mixed with Turpenoid among the yellow dots.
- **Roses and variegated primroses**. With burnt sienna, paint an open circle on each rose, then add some curved lines in a spiral around this, followed by some dots. At the very center, add a dot of chromium oxide green that has been thinned with Turpenoid. Define the outer edge of each primrose center with burnt sienna, and add a dot of red at the very center.
- **Bluets**. Add a dot of alizarin crimson mixed with Turpenoid at the center of each bluet.
- **Vase and alabaster**. Paint the curving lines on the vase using a mix of Payne's gray and Turpenoid.
- **Alabaster**. With a mix of Payne's gray, Prussian blue, and Turpenoid, paint fine random lines for veins in the stone.
- **Stems, thorns, and leaf veins**. Mix a little greenish umber with some chromium oxide green and Turpenoid. Using this green mixture, paint curved lines for the stems. Paint in the leaf veins with a darker mixture than used for the stems. With quick, little strokes, paint some tiny lines to represent thorns on the roses. On the daisy, add a few green dots to the dots of transparent gold ochre and burnt sienna.

# Memorial Theorem

This style of memorial art was common at the end of the eighteenth century and into the nineteenth (see page 14). A number of the surviving examples of memorial art are needlework pieces that were executed by young ladies at their academies, with some embellishments usually hand-painted by the schoolmaster. A number of memorial paintings were done in remembrance of George Washington. I created this theorem, picturing Mount Vernon overlooking the countryside, at the request of Mr. and Mrs. Walt Henderson of Leesburg, Virginia.

## Palette

- yellow ochre
- burnt sienna
- alizarin crimson
- Grumbacher red
- chromium oxide green
- greenish umber
- sap green
- Prussian blue
- burnt umber
- Payne's gray
- Davy's gray
- ivory black
- Permalba white
- Liquin
- Turpenoid

If you would like to make this theorem as a personal memorial for a loved one, you can replace Mount Vernon with the church that is included above. The quote on the tombstone depicted here is one attributed to George Washington, but you can replace it with any other quote you like. Enlarge the drawings 130 percent for an 11 x 11-inch frame. Before mixing your colors, review the instructions on Mixing Liquin and Paints on page 17. Practice writing the quote on several scraps of velvet before adding it to your theorem.

### MIXING COLORS
- **Mountains**. Mix two colors for the hills and mountains. First blend alizarin crimson, Prussian blue, and Payne's gray to create a purple. To one-third of this purple mixture, add some greenish umber to make a greenish purple.
- **Sky**. For the sky, mix two pale colors. To a puddle of Liquin about the size of a nickel, add a dot of Prussian blue. Check this sky color on a scrap of velvet and adjust if necessary. To another nickel-size puddle of Liquin, add some alizarin crimson to make a pink sky color. Check this color as before.

- **Blue dress**. To a dime-size puddle of Liquin, add a dot of Prussian blue. This blue should be slightly deeper in value than the sky color.
- **Flesh**. To some Permalba white, add a dot of yellow ochre, mixing well. Then add a dot of burnt sienna and mix again. Adjust the color with tiny amounts of Grumbacher red.
- **Monument**. To a nickel-size puddle of Liquin, add a little Payne's gray.
- **Bushes**. Mix a dark blue-green by adding a little Prussian blue to some greenish umber.

### PAINTING THE SKY
Before beginning the stencil work, you need to paint the sky. Start by picking up some of the pink sky color with the largest stencil brush. Paint some of the pink here and there in the sky, leaving spaces unpainted for white clouds and blue areas. With another large, round scrubber brush, pick up some of the blue sky color. Paint blue areas in the sky, leaving unpainted spaces of the velvet to represent soft, white clouds. Be careful not to blend the pink and blue, or you will have purple areas in the sky.

### STENCIL NUMBER 1
- **Flesh**. Paint the edges of the lady's arm and the angel's leg with the flesh mixture, leaving the centers light. Place the small, rounded end of a curve on the angel where the arm joins the body. Shade lightly along this curve with burnt sienna. Paint the tummy of the angel, creating a shadow under the arm area. Shade the rest of the angel along the edges, keeping the center of the body and arm light. Place the rounded end of a curve over each face, matching the curve with the point where the chin meets the neck, and shade with a little burnt sienna.
- **Urn and monument**. Paint along the edges of the urn and monument pieces with the Payne's gray–Liquin mixture, fading quickly to the color of the velvet.
- **Mount Vernon and sails on boat**. Paint the house and boat sails with Permalba white.
- **Stream**. Paint some Payne's gray along the top area of the water. Paint the stream with a very light coat of Prussian blue, rendering the water with uneven shades of blue.
- **Tree trunks**. Paint the tree trunks with burnt sienna, making the edges darker.
- **Blades of grass**. Base-paint the blades of grass with yellow ochre, then shade with chromium oxide green.
- **Treetops**. Base-paint the leaves of the treetops with yellow ochre, then shade with chromium oxide green, making the color uneven.

## STENCIL NUMBER 2

- **Flesh**. Paint along the edges of the angel's arms and legs with the flesh color, keeping the center light. Paint the lady's arm with the flesh color.
- **River**. Paint the river with a light value of Prussian blue, starting at the top and fading out toward the bottom.
- **Lady's dress**. Paint the edges of the skirt and sleeve with the Prussian blue–Liquin mixture. On the skirt, shade some curvy areas to create the look of folds in the fabric.
- **Urn**. Paint the edges of the urn pieces with the Payne's gray–Liquin mixture, leaving the center of the urn the color of the velvet.
- **Stream bank**. Paint a light value of burnt umber along just the top edge of the stream bank.
- **Lawn and treetops**. Base-paint the lawn and treetops with yellow ochre, then shade unevenly with chromium oxide green.
- **Angel's wing and drapery**. Paint along the edges of the wings and drapery on the angel with Davy's gray.
- **Bush**. Base-paint the bush with yellow ochre, making this color uneven, then shade unevenly with chromium oxide of green. Shade the edges lightly with a little of the Prussian blue–greenish umber mix.
- **Tree**. Base-paint the trunk of the tree with burnt sienna. Shade the left edge of the tree and top edge of the branches with burnt umber.

## STENCIL NUMBER 3

- **Dress bodice**. Paint the dress bodice with the Prussian blue–Liquin mixture. Shade the underarm of the sleeve and under the bust a darker value of the Prussian blue–Liquin mixture.
- **Hankie**. Paint the hankie with Permalba white.
- **Monument and urn**. Paint the edges of the monument with the Payne's gray–Liquin mixture, fading quickly to the color of the velvet. Paint along the edges of the urn top with the Payne's gray–Liquin mixture.
- **Tree leaves and grass blades**. Base-paint the leaves and grass blades in yellow ochre, then shade along the edges with chromium oxide green.
- **Boat**. Paint the boat with burnt umber.
- **Roof**. Use Payne's gray for the roof.
- **Front door**. The door is done with Grumbacher red.
- **Bush**. Base-paint the bush with yellow ochre, then shade unevenly with chromium oxide green. Paint along the lower right side with the Prussian blue–greenish umber mixture.
- **Lawn**. Base-paint the lawn unevenly with yellow ochre, and then shade with chromium oxide green,

making the green uneven as well. Place an undulating curve to the right of the lady on the lawn. Shade this curve with the Prussian blue–greenish umber mixture, creating a dip in the lawn. Use the same color to shade the bank and lower edge of the lawn.

## STENCIL NUMBER 4

- **Monument pieces**. Paint along the edges on the left with the Payne's gray–Liquin mixture.
- **Lawn and grass blades**. Base-paint the lawn and blades of grass with yellow ochre, then shade with chromium oxide green, applying the lawn colors unevenly.
- **Tree on right**. Base-paint the trunk of the tree with burnt sienna. Shade the left edge of the tree and top edge of the branches with burnt umber.
- **Mountains and hill**. Place the saved hill piece in the stencil opening, and secure with a small piece of tape. Paint the top of the mountain with the purple mixture, fading out about one-third down. Blend the greenish purple mixture into the purple, starting where the purple fades out. Carefully paint this color around the cypress trees. Remove the hill piece, and place the saved mountain piece over the purple mountain. Base-paint the hill with yellow ochre. Shade the left side of the hill with the greenish purple mixture, fading this color out on the other side of the lady's head. From the right side of the hill, shade the hill with chromium oxide green, blending into the greenish mountain color.

> ### Tips for Writing on Velvet
>
> - Mix some Payne's gray and Turpenoid together. Then add a drop of Skin So Soft to the mixture. Test the color on a scrap of velvet. If the color is too light, add more Payne's gray and test the color again. Keep the mixture watery.
> - Keep the brush vertical. Only allow the tip of the brush to touch the surface. Elevate the heel of your hand so you have free movement for your writing.
> - Practice writing the quote on paper towels before trying to write on velvet. Follow this by writing the passage several times on a scrap piece of velvet.
> - Cover any painted areas with paper towels. This keeps the painted areas from smudging when writing quotes on the monument.

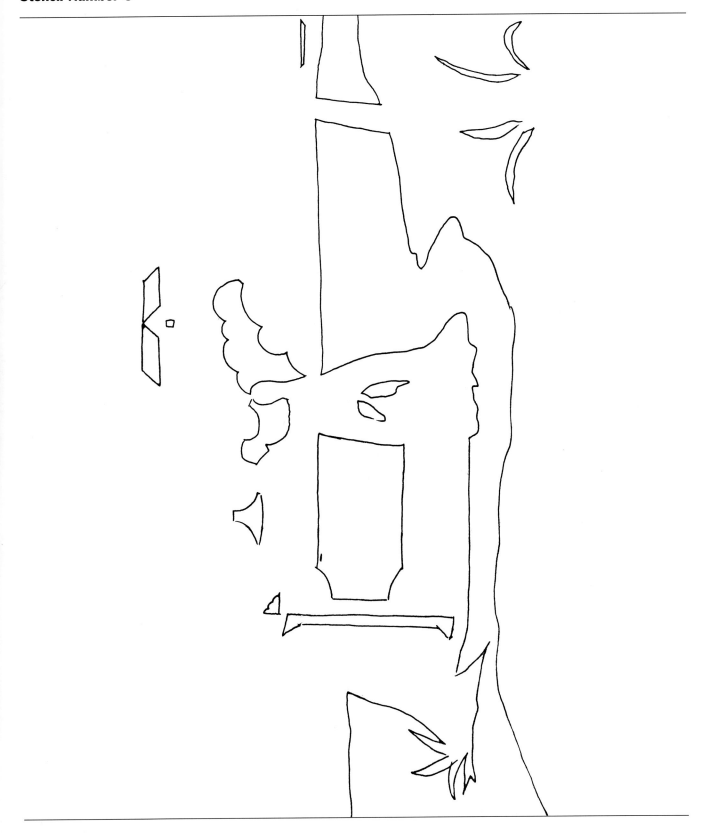

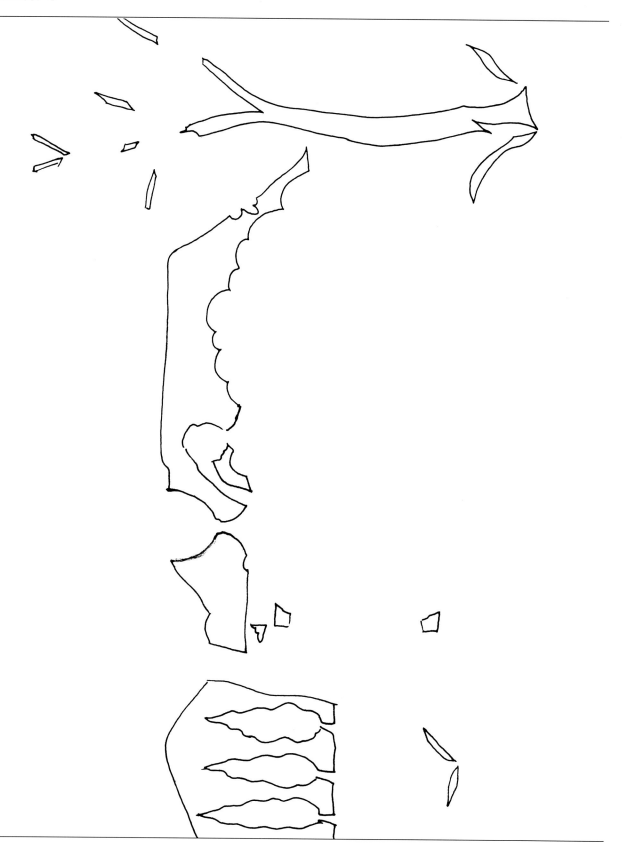

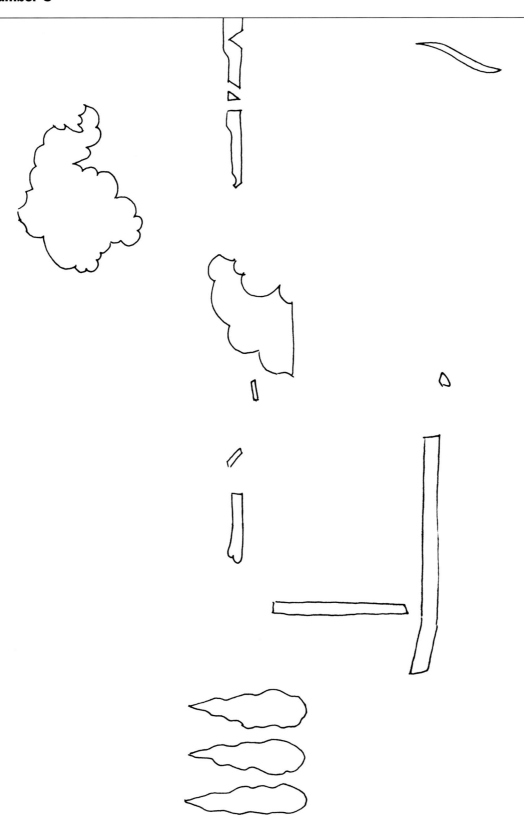

## Design Notes for Stencils

- Trace and cut the cupola and house on stencil number 1.
- Trace and cut the cupola roof on stencil number 2.
- Trace and cut the roof and door on stencil number 3.
- Trace and cut the sleeve cuff on stencil number 5.

### STENCIL NUMBER 5

- **Base of urn and foot of monument**. Paint the upper edge of the foot of the monument with the Payne's gray–Liquin mixture. Place a curve in the middle of the foot of the urn to cover the lower half, lining it up with the point. Then shade the urn foot along the edge of the curve with the same paint.
- **Cuffs of sleeves**. Paint the sleeve cuffs with Prussian blue.
- **Bush**. Base-paint the bush with yellow ochre, then shade unevenly with chromium oxide green. Shade the right side of the bush with the Prussian blue–greenish umber mixture.
- **Tree leaves and grass blades**. Base-paint the leaves and grass blades with yellow ochre, then shade with chromium oxide green.
- **Cypress trees and treetops**. Base-paint the cypress trees and treetops with yellow ochre, then shade unevenly with chromium oxide green. Shade the edges of the cypress trees with the Prussian blue–greenish umber mixture.
- **Hills on other side of river**. Paint the top of the hills with the purple mountain color and the lower edge with the greenish purple mixture. Keep these values light because the hills are in the distance.
- **Shoe**. Paint the shoe with ivory black.

### DETAIL

- **Body parts, faces, and hair**. Mix Turpenoid and burnt sienna, and add a drop of Skin So Soft oil. With the liner brush, use this mixture to outline the arms, legs, and lady's profile. Paint the features on the faces, and finish with the hair.
- **Flag on boat**. Mix some Grumbacher red and Turpenoid to paint a flag at the top of the sail.
- **Monument, urn, sails, and house**. Paint all detail on the monument, urn, sails, and house with Payne's gray mixed with Turpenoid, following the lines on the drawing.
- **Quote on monument**. Use the same Payne's gray mixture for the quote on the monument.
- **Angel wings, drapery, and hankie**. Again following the drawing, paint the detail on the angel's wings, drapery, and hankie with the Payne's gray mixture.
- **Folds in dress**. Paint some lines to create folds in the dress with Prussian blue mixed with Turpenoid and Skin So Soft oil.
- **Branches on left tree**. With a mixture of burnt sienna and Turpenoid, paint fine lines to create thin branches and connect the leaves to the stenciled branches.
- **Curls in treetops, bushes, cypress trees, and thin blades of grass**. Deepen the greenish purple mountain color with some greenish umber and mix in some Turpenoid. Use this mixture to paint curls in the treetops on the right, larger curls on the bushes, and tiny curls on the cypress trees.

# Basket of Fruit

Fruit baskets are a favorite of mine. This theorem is a reflection of our bountiful world and the beauty we live with every day. You may feel a sense of excitement when painting a large piece for the first time, and your efforts will be well rewarded with this lovely design. Enlarge the drawing 175 percent for a perfect fit in a 16 x 20-inch frame. Either a grain-painted or gilded frame works well with this piece.

152

## Palette

- transparent gold ochre
- yellow ochre
- Indian yellow
- burnt sienna
- alizarin crimson
- alizarin crimson golden
- Grumbacher red
- chromium oxide green
- greenish umber
- sap green
- Prussian blue
- burnt umber
- Turpenoid

## Tips

- Cut curves for the stem areas of the pears and the cherries. Cut curves for the peaches on stencils number 2 and 3.
- Cut the saved leaves along the dotted lines, and mark each of these pieces with the stencil number.
- Cut a triangle to be used on the pineapple sections.

### MIXING COLORS

- **Pineapple leaves**. Mix chromium oxide green with some greenish umber. Add a little Prussian blue to deepen the green mixture.

### STENCIL NUMBER 1

- **Pear**. Base-paint the pear with Indian yellow. Paint a very pale wash of sap green over the complete pear, making the edges a deeper value. Place the half of the curve with the bump in the center at the base of the stem position. Shade the pear along the curve line with transparent gold ochre, fading out the paint so there is no harsh line. Remove the curve, and shade the very top edge of the pear and along the sides with the same paint. Deepen the lower edge of the pear with a very pale shading of burnt sienna. Then use alizarin crimson to paint a light blush on the lower side of the pear and on the right side at the top and under the stem.
- **Pineapple sections**. Base-paint the pineapple sections with Indian yellow. Shade the edges with transparent gold ochre, keeping the center light, and then with burnt sienna. Make a light stroke of chromium oxide green from the top toward the center of each section. Place the triangular stencil in the center of a section, then shade this triangle with burnt sienna, fading out toward the bottom. Do not paint a complete triangle; it is important to fade as directed so the pineapple looks real.

Pineapple sections along the edge of the fruit are at an angle; place the triangle on an angle as well. If the jagged edges of a leaf overlap a section of fruit, place the triangle over the jagged leaf edge and continue stenciling as if the section were whole.

- **Cut ends of branches and pear stems**. Base-paint the cut ends of both the branches and pear stems with yellow ochre.
- **Cherries**. Base-paint the cherries with Grumbacher red. Place the curve with a bump in position on one of the cherries, then shade the cherry on the edges and along the curve with alizarin crimson. Repeat on the other cherry. Remove the curve, and shade the top edge of the cherry.
- **Peach**. Base-paint the peach with Indian yellow. Paint the edge of the left side of the peach with transparent gold ochre, then shade with alizarin crimson golden. The right side should be a very pale yellow.

- **Basket**. Base-paint the basket with yellow ochre. The brush strokes should go from side to side, with the deepest value on the edges. Paint the basket with burnt sienna, again brushing from side to side, with the deepest value on the side edges. With burnt umber, shade the side edges of the basket, and then along the bottom and behind the strawberries.
- **Left grape leaf**. Base-paint the grape leaf on the left with yellow ochre. Paint the tips on the left and upper right with burnt sienna. Shade the leaf very lightly with chromium oxide green. The deeper green shade on the leaf is done with a later stencil.
- **Right and center cherry leaves**. Base-paint these leaves with yellow ochre. Shade the tips on the center leaf with burnt sienna. Shade the leaves with chromium oxide green. Then shade the portion that is behind another leaf with some Prussian blue.
- **Pineapple leaves**. Base-paint the pineapple leaves with yellow ochre, then shade with the pineapple leaf mixture. Deepen the value along the edge of the area that is behind another leaf.
- **Grapes**. Base-paint the grapes with Prussian blue, making the grapes appear round by darkening the edges and keeping the centers light. Deepen any areas that are behind or shadowed by another grape.

**STENCIL NUMBER 2**

- **Pear**. Base-paint the pear with Indian yellow. Paint a very pale wash of sap green over the complete pear, making the edges and the left side a deeper value. Place the half of the curve with the bump in the center at the base of the stem position. Shade the pear along the curve line with transparent gold ochre. Remove the curve, and shade the edges of the pear with this same color. Shade the bottom portion of the pear with a little burnt sienna and then burnt umber.
- **Pineapple sections**. Base-paint the sections with Indian yellow, then shade the edges with transparent gold ochre, keeping the very center light. Shade the edges with some burnt sienna. Use a light stroke of chromium oxide green from the top toward the center of each section.

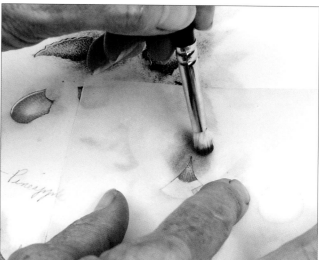

Place the triangular stencil in the center of a section, then shade this triangle with burnt sienna, fading out toward the bottom. Along the edge of the fruit, where the pineapple sections are at an angle, place the triangle on an angle as well.

Watch for the left two pineapple sections, which might be mistaken for grapes. Repeat this process on the remaining sections.

**Stencil Number 3**

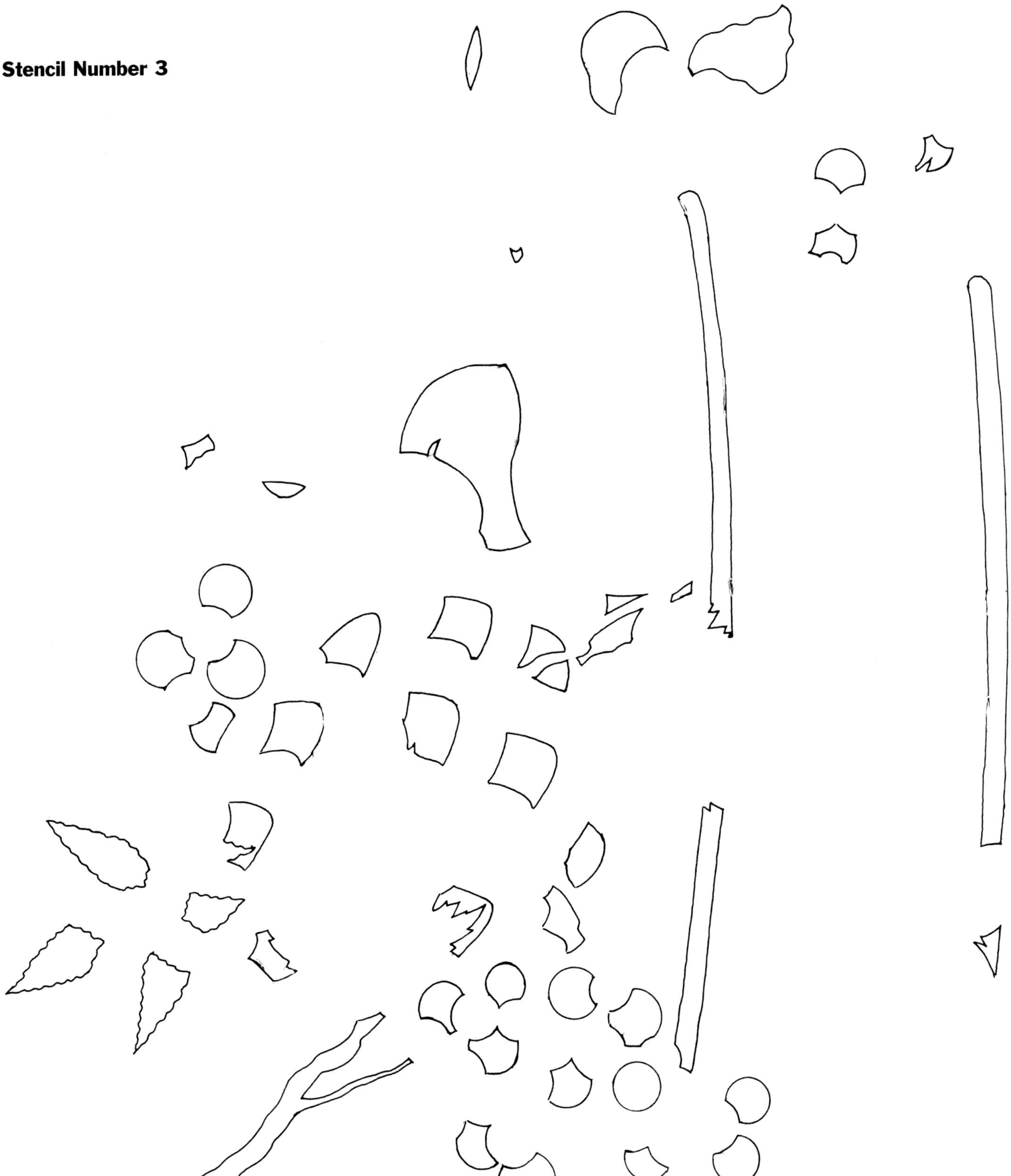

- **Cherry**. Lightly base-paint the cherry with Grumbacher red. Place the curve with the bump in position on the cherry. Shade the cherry on the edges and along the curve with alizarin crimson. Remove the curve, and use the same color to shade the very top of the cherry.
- **Pineapple leaves**. Base-paint the leaves of the pineapple with yellow ochre, then shade with the pineapple leaf mixture. Deepen areas that are behind another leaf.
- **Grapes**. Base-paint the grapes with Prussian blue, making the grapes appear round by darkening the edges and keeping the centers light. Deepen any areas that are behind or shadowed by another grape.
- **Peach**. Base-paint the peach with Indian yellow. Place the concave curve on the peach, and shade the edges with transparent gold ochre, keeping the center light. With the curve still in place, shade with alizarin crimson golden. Deepen the top edge of the peach that is tucked behind the other two peaches with a little burnt umber. Remove the curve, and shade the lower half with transparent gold ochre and then alizarin crimson golden.
- **Branch and basket rims**. Base-paint the branch and basket rims with yellow ochre, then shade with burnt sienna. Now shade the lower portions with burnt umber. This gives the branch and basket rims a rounded appearance.
- **Left grape leaf**. Place the left portion of the saved leaf piece into position. Shade the leaf along the upper part and the lower right side of the opening with chromium oxide green, followed by some Prussian blue. Remove the left leaf piece, and place the right portion into position. Shade along the vein side and upper edge, then overshade this area with a little Prussian blue.
- **Leaf on right**. This leaf is completed on two stencils. Base-paint the leaf with yellow ochre, then shade with a very light value of chromium oxide green.

**STENCIL NUMBER 3**
- **Peach**. Base-paint the peach with Indian yellow. Place the concave curve on the peach, then shade the edges with transparent gold ochre, keeping the center and lower edge light. Fade out along the curve $3/8$ inch from the bottom of the peach. Keeping the curve in place, shade along the curve and under the top peach with alizarin crimson golden, fading out as with the transparent gold ochre. Add a little burnt umber in the area under the top peach to define the two peaches. Remove the curve, and shade the top edge with transparent gold ochre, then alizarin crimson golden.

- **Pineapple sections**. Base-paint the sections with Indian yellow, then shade the edges with transparent gold ochre, keeping the very center light. Shade the edges with some burnt sienna. Use a light stroke of chromium oxide green from the top toward the center of each section.

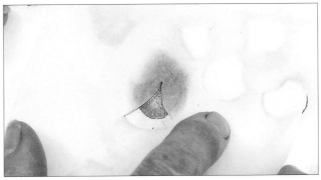

Place the triangular stencil in the center of a section, then shade this triangle with burnt sienna, fading out toward the bottom. Remember to angle the positioning of the triangle as you work through the pineapple.

Repeat this process with the triangle on the remaining sections.

- **Leaf on right side**. Deepen the area along the lower edge and left side with chromium oxide green, followed by a hint of Prussian blue.
- **Branches and basket rims**. Base-paint the branches and basket rims with yellow ochre, and then shade with burnt sienna. Then shade these lower portions with burnt umber.
- **Pear stems**. Paint the pear stems yellow ochre, then shade with burnt sienna, keeping the centers a lighter brown.
- **Grapes**. Base-paint the grapes with Prussian blue, making the grapes appear round by darkening the edges and keeping the centers light. Deepen any areas that are behind or shadowed by another grape.
- **Pineapple leaves**. Base-paint the leaves of the pineapple with yellow ochre, then shade with the pineapple leaf mixture, deepening any areas that are behind another leaf.
- **Cherry**. Base-paint the cherry lightly with Grumbacher red. Place the curve with the bump in position on the cherry, then shade the edges of the cherry and along the curve with alizarin crimson. Remove the curve, and use the same color to shade along the top edge. Deepen the lower area that is behind the other cherries.
- **Leaf on left of basket**. Base-paint this leaf with yellow ochre, then shade with chromium oxide green, keeping the tip a lighter value. Deepen the green along the right side and under the grape.
- **Background in basket**. Base-paint this area with yellow ochre, then shade a medium dark green using the pineapple leaf color mixture. If this is not dark enough after you have painted the leaves, put the stencil back on and deepen the color.

**STENCIL NUMBER 4**
- **Peach**. Base-paint the large peach half with Indian yellow. Shade the sides with transparent gold ochre, keeping the center light, and then with alizarin crimson golden.
- **Small peach along basket rim**. Base-paint the peach with Indian yellow. Shade the edges of the peach with transparent gold ochre, keeping the center light, and then with alizarin crimson golden.
- **Pineapple leaf**. Base-paint the leaf of the pineapple with yellow ochre; then shade with the pineapple leaf mixture, making the area behind the other leaves a deeper value.
- **Grapes**. Base-paint the grapes with Prussian blue, making the grapes appear round by darkening the edges and keeping the centers light. Deepen any areas that are behind or shadowed by another grape.

- **Grape leaf on lower right**. Base-paint the leaf with yellow ochre, then shade the tips with some burnt sienna. Place the saved lower grape leaf piece into the opening. Shade the upper portion with chromium oxide green, deepening the value along the center edge of the leaf piece. Remove this piece, and shade the rest of the leaf with chromium oxide green.
- **Other leaves and strawberry hulls**. Base-paint the leaves and strawberry hulls with yellow ochre. Shade the leaves with chromium oxide green, keeping the tips a lighter green. Using a curved shield, paint along the edges with chromium oxide green. Move the shield to shade each section of the hulls.
- **Branch and basket rim**. Base-paint the branch and basket rim with yellow ochre, then shade with burnt sienna. Then shade these lower portions with burnt umber.
- **Pineapple sections**. Base-paint the pineapple sections with Indian yellow, then shade the edges with transparent gold ochre, keeping the very center light. Shade the edges with some burnt sienna. Use a light stroke of chromium oxide green from the top toward the center of each section.

**Stencil Number 5**

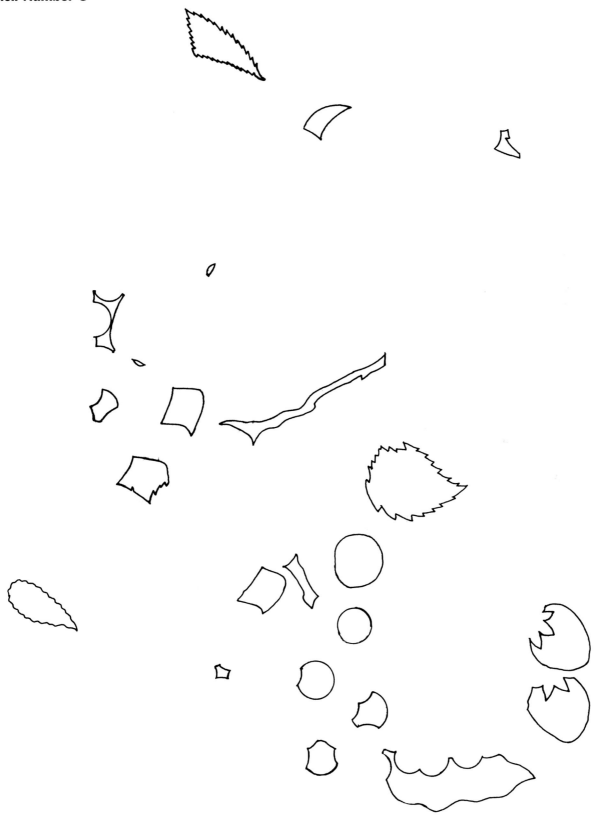

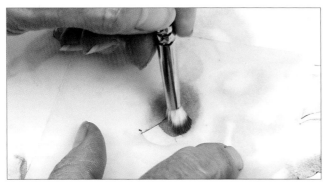

Place the triangular stencil in the center of a section, then shade this triangle with burnt sienna, fading out toward the bottom.

Repeat this process on the remaining sections.

- **Strawberry**. Paint the strawberry with alizarin crimson, making the area under the hull a darker value.

**STENCIL NUMBER 5**

- **Pineapple sections**. Base-paint the pineapple sections with Indian yellow. Shade the edges with transparent gold ochre, keeping the very center light, and then with some burnt sienna. Make a light stroke of chromium oxide green from the top toward the center of each section.

Place the triangular stencil in the center of a section, then shade this triangle with burnt sienna, fading out toward the bottom.

Repeat this process on the remaining sections.

- **Grapes**. Base-paint the grapes with Prussian blue, making the grapes appear round by darkening the edges and keeping the centers light. Deepen any areas that are behind or shadowed by another grape.
- **Strawberries**. Paint the strawberries with alizarin crimson, making the areas under the hulls a darker value. Also deepen the value along the bottom of the strawberry on the left and the right side of the berry on the right.
- **Cherry**. Base-paint the cherry with Grumbacher red. Place the curve with the bump in position on the cherry, then shade the cherry on the edges and along the curve with alizarin crimson. Remove the curve, and use the same color to shade along the top edge. Deepen the lower area of the cherry that is behind the other cherries.
- **Branches**. Base-paint with yellow ochre, then shade the branches with burnt sienna. Next shade along the edges of these lower portions with burnt umber.
- **Peach half at basket rim**. Base-paint the peach half with Indian yellow. Shade the outer edge of the peach with transparent gold ochre, then with alizarin crimson golden. Leave the area near the previously painted half yellow.
- **Peach stem ends**. Paint only along the edges with burnt umber.
- **Pineapple leaf**. Base-paint the leaf of the pineapple with yellow ochre, then shade with the pineapple leaf blue mixture.
- **Leaf in center of basket**. Base-paint the leaf with yellow ochre, then shade the tips with burnt sienna. Put the left portion of the saved leaf pieces in place. Shade the leaf with chromium oxide green, deepening the

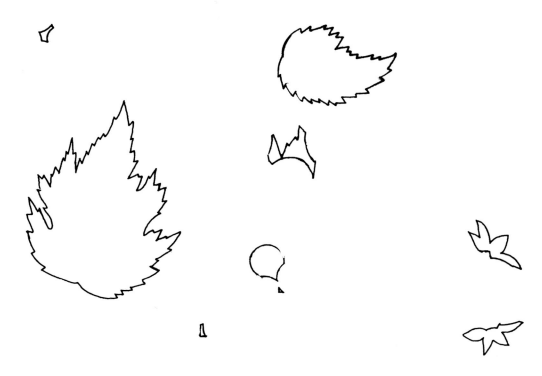

value along the center edge of the leaf piece. Remove the leaf piece, and use this same color to shade the remainder of the leaf.

- **Leaf on left**. Base-paint the leaf with yellow ochre, then shade with chromium oxide green. Paint the area on the right next to the grapes a darker value.

### STENCIL NUMBER 6

- **Triangle between peach on basket rim and lower pear**. Paint this triangle with the pineapple leaf mixture.
- **Grapes**. Base-paint the grapes with Prussian blue, making them appear round by darkening the edges and keeping the centers light. Deepen any area that is behind another grape. The small odd shapes are portions of recessed grapes that are behind all the other grapes. Paint these shapes a dark blue.
- **Strawberry hulls**. Base-paint the hulls with yellow ochre. Use a curved shield, and paint along the edge with chromium oxide green. Move the shield to shade each section of the hulls.

### Design Notes for Stencils

- When tracing the stencils, save all items marked "SAVE."
- Trace the dotted lines on the pieces marked "SAVE."
- When cutting a saved stencil piece, cut along the line and save both pieces.
- The left grape leaf is painted on two different stencils. Save only the cutting of this leaf marked with the circled number 2.
- Trace and cut the curves for the peaches, cherries, and pears.
- Cut a 4-inch square of stencil film. On this square, trace and cut the triangle to use for accent painting on the pineapple.

- **Grape leaf**. Base-paint the leaf with yellow ochre, then shade the tips with some burnt umber. Place the upper half of the grape leaf into the opening. Shade the leaf with chromium oxide green, making the area along the center vein a darker value. Remove the piece, and use the same color to shade the rest of the leaf.
- **Center leaf**. Base-paint the leaf and triangle with yellow ochre. Place the right side piece of the leaf back in the opening, and shade with chromium oxide green. Remove the piece, and paint the rest of the leaf with the same color. Correct any "holidays" at this time before proceeding with the detail.

## DETAIL
- **Cut ends of branches, stems, and peach end**. Mix some Turpenoid with a little burnt sienna, and paint fine lines to outline these items. Paint some fine lines in an oval shape in the inside of each of the branch ends.
- **Cherry stems**. Paint fine lines for the cherry stems with the same mixture, starting at the branches and moving toward the cherry.

- **Pineapple sections**. Paint fine lines with the mixture in a star pattern from the point of the triangle toward the outside of each pineapple section. Do not go completely to the edge of the pineapple sections.
- **Strawberry seeds**. Mix a little burnt umber with some alizarin crimson, and add some Turpenoid. Paint some dots on the strawberries to represent seeds.
- **Basket rim detail**. Mix burnt sienna with some burnt umber, and add some Turpenoid. Paint elongated S-shaped lines to create roping in the rim pieces.
- **Leaf veins and grape tendrils**. Mix a little greenish umber with some chromium oxide green to make a medium-value green. Add some Turpenoid, and paint the veins of the leaves and the tendrils. If the veining in the leaves does not show up, deepen the green with more greenish umber.
- **Center veins in pineapple leaves**. Add a little Prussian blue to deepen the pineapple leaf mixture, and add some Turpenoid. Paint a wiggly line down the center of each pineapple leaf.
- **Grass**. When the painting is dry, mix yellow ochre with a touch of chromium oxide green to make a yellow-green, then add some transparent gold ochre. Use a large brush to paint a light green ground.

# Blue Vase of Flowers

Project 9

This very graceful vase of flowers was originally painted about 1800 by a young lady named Sarah Wilson, daughter of Captain David and Sarah (Davis) Wilson (see page 10). The family lived in Philadelphia. The antique painting was a gift from a friend and teacher of mine, Jane Bolster. Because of the age of the painting by Miss Wilson, a lot of foxing—discoloring of the velvet—and fading have occurred, but the colors have been carefully matched. This is a lovely piece to paint. Enlarge the drawing 189 percent for an 18 x 18-inch frame.

165

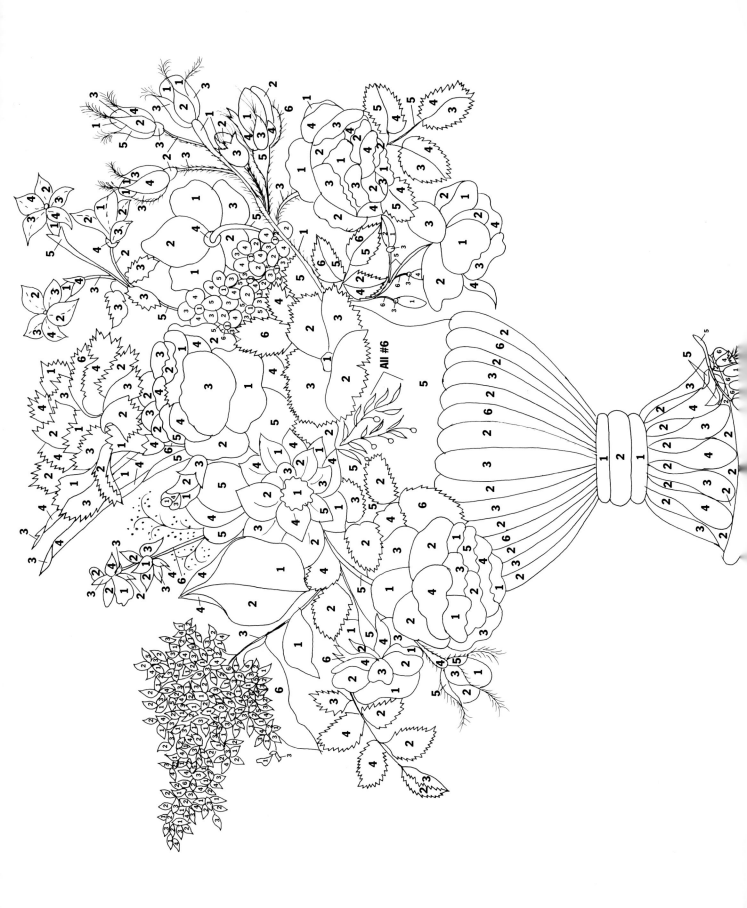

## Palette

- transparent gold ochre
- raw sienna
- cadmium yellow light
- alizarin crimson
- alizarin crimson golden
- chromium oxide green
- Prussian blue
- cerulean blue
- raw umber
- Payne's gray
- Permalba white

## Tips

- Use a paper punch for the tiny round flowers.
- Cut several small curves for defining the blue flowers on the right.
- Raw umber is a browner yellow than yellow ochre and looks good on tips of leaves.
- Check the depth of the colors on a scrap of velvet and adjust if necessary.
- Use the Liquin only where specified.

## MIXING COLORS

- **Carnation**. Mix a little transparent gold ochre with some alizarin crimson golden to make a beautiful salmon pink. Mix a good amount and divide into two portions. Keep half for the carnation, and use the other half for the pink rose color.
- **White roses**. Mix Liquin with some Payne's gray, making a pale gray.
- **Pink rose**. To one portion of the salmon pink, add some Liquin to create a soft pale pink.
- **Forget-me-nots**. Mix a dot of Prussian blue with some cerulean blue to temper it. Divide the resulting blue in half. Add some Liquin to one portion to lighten it a bit for the forget-me-nots, and use the other half to mix the color for the lilacs and blue flowers.

- **Lilacs and blue flowers**. To the other half of the blue mixture, add a bit more Prussian blue to make a different value than for the forget-me-nots. Then mix in a touch of Payne's gray.
- **Blue vase**. Mix cerulean blue with a small amount of Prussian blue, and add a little raw umber. Be careful not to add too much raw umber, or it can turn the mixture green.
- **Yellow flowers**. Mix a little cadmium yellow light with some Permalba white, creating a pale yellow. Divide this color in half, and use one portion for the yellow flowers and the other to mix the base color for the vase.
- **Vase base color**. To one half of the yellow mixture, add more of the white to make a very pale yellow.

## STENCIL NUMBER 1

- **Lilac**. Paint each of the lilac petals a very pale blue using the lilac color. Shade only one side of these along the edge a darker value.
- **Centers of blue flowers**. Paint with cadmium yellow light.
- **Blue flowers**. Base-paint the petals of the blue flowers with the lilac blue color. Paint the flowers on the left a deeper value of the lilac color than the flowers on the right. Shade the larger petal on the left a darker value along the bottom. Place a curve in the center of the petal on the right, and shade along the curve. On the top blue flower on the right, deepen the petal at the top edge and fade to the bottom.
- **White roses**. On the large rose, lightly paint the top petal along the edge with the Payne's gray–Liquin mixture. Fade off quickly to the velvet color. Shade the bottom edge of this petal, then switch to a smaller brush and paint a gentle fold on the petal. Paint the other three petals along the top edge only. On the smaller rose, shade along the left side of the large petal, quickly fading to the velvet color, and deepen the right side. Shade along the lower edges and sides of the top petal, then shade just the left side of the remaining petal.
- **White rosebud**. With the same mixture, shade the top edge and lightly shade the outer edge.
- **Forget-me-nots centers**. Paint the centers of the forget-me-nots with cadmium yellow light, then shade the lower portions with transparent gold ochre.

167

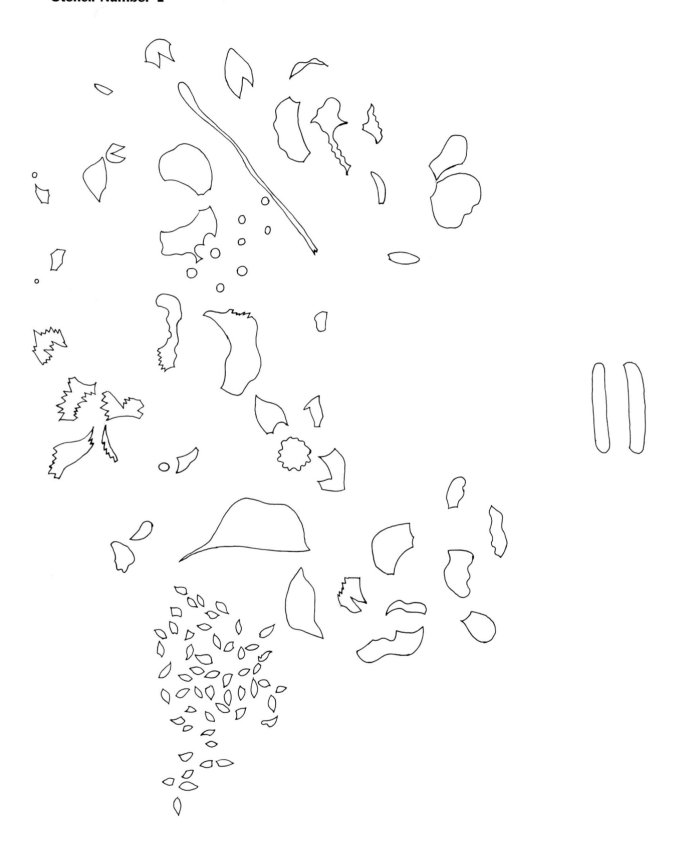

- **Yellow flowers on right**. Lightly base-paint the petals of these two flowers with the yellow mixture, keeping the centers of the petals light. On the top flower, shade the right side of the left petal, and then the left side of the right petal with transparent gold ochre. On the lower flower, shade the right petal along the top and right side with transparent gold ochre. With a small brush, shade a curved shape on the large petal from the bottom toward the center.

- **Carnation**. Lightly base-paint the petals of the carnation with the salmon pink mixture. Starting on the left side of the flower, shade the first petal along the left side and bottom a deeper value. Then shade the lower left petal along the lower edge darker. Shade the top center petal along the lower edge and right side. On the right top petal, shade along the lower edges a darker value. Overshade the pink on the lower center petal with chromium oxide green, then the edges with Prussian blue. Use the Prussian blue sparingly.

- **Red rose**. Base-paint the rose petals with alizarin crimson, keeping the center of the petals light. Shade along the upper edges of the lower petal and the bottom edge of the top petal.

- **Red rosebud**. Shade the center petal with alizarin crimson along the lower edge.

- **Yellow double daffodil**. Lightly base-paint the petals and the center with the yellow mixture. Place the rounded side of a curve on a petal, and shade along the edge of the curve to create the fold in the petal. Move the curve for each petal marked on the pattern with a curved line.

- **Pink rosebuds**. Base-paint the pink rosebuds with the salmon pink–Liquin mixture along the outer edge of the stencil, fading to white toward the calyx.

- **Pink rose**. Base-paint the rose petals with a very light value of the same mixture, keeping the centers light. Deepen the top petal on the lower edge. With a small stencil brush, shade two folds in the top petal. Then shade along the upper edge of the center petal, the top edge of the lower petal, and the outer edge of the petal on the right.

- **Stem, calyx of red rose, and yellow buds on right**. Base-paint the stem with raw sienna, then shade the edges with chromium oxide green, keeping the center light. Base-paint and shade the red rose calyx and yellow flower buds on the right with the same two colors.

- **Center of white dianthus**. Base-paint the dianthus center with raw sienna, then shade the edges with chromium oxide green.

- **Vase**. Lightly base-paint the center of the vase pieces with the pale yellow mixture, then shade the edges with the blue vase mixture.

- **Lily of the valley**. With the Payne's gray–Liquin mixture, shade along the edges of these flowers, fading to the velvet color quickly.

- **Lilac leaves**. Base-paint the leaves with raw sienna. Shade the leaves with chromium oxide green, leaving some of the raw sienna showing. Overshade the green in the center of the smaller leaf with Prussian blue. Overshade the green on the large leaf along the left side with Prussian blue.

## STENCIL NUMBER 2

- **Lilac**. Lightly base-paint the petals of the lilac with the lilac blue mixture, then shade the edges a darker value.

- **Blue flowers on left**. Lightly base-paint the petals of the blue flowers with the lilac blue color. Then shade the right side of the top and bottom flower petals on the left, and the left side of the top and bottom petals on the right.

- **Blue flowers on right**. Lightly base-paint the petals of the blue flowers with the lilac blue color. Paint a fold in the petals of the flowers on the right, using the round side of a curve. Refer to the dotted lines on the drawing as a guide.

- **Yellow flowers on right**. Base-paint the petals of these two flowers with the yellow flower mixture, keeping the centers light. On the top flower, use transparent gold ochre to shade the top petal along the upper edge and the lower petal along the upper edge and sides. On the bottom flower, shade the left petal on the lower edge, the top right petal along the upper edge, and the lower right petal on the left edge.

- **White roses and rosebud**. On the large rose, shade along the lower edges of the top two petals with the Payne's gray–Liquin mixture. Fade quickly to the velvet color. Shade along the top edge only of the lower petal. On the smaller rose, shade the upper edge of the top petal and fade quickly into the center of the petal. Then shade along the top and bottom edges of the lower petal. On the white rosebud, shade the lower curved edge.

- **Carnation.** Lightly base-paint the petals of the carnation with the salmon pink mixture. Shade the lower edges of the top two petals and the right and left lower petals on the right and left sides along the lower edges. Then shade the top of the center lower petal, fading out toward the center.
- **Yellow double daffodil.** Lightly base-paint the petals with the yellow flower color. Place a curve in the center of the top petal, and shade along the edge with transparent gold ochre. Then shade each of the other petals, using the curved lines on the drawing for placement of the shield.
- **Red rose.** Base-paint the rose petals with alizarin crimson, keeping the center of the petals light. Then shade the lower edge of the top three petals, the right side of the left petal, and the left side of the petal on the right a darker value.
- **White dianthus.** With the Payne's gray–Liquin mixture, shade along the lower edge of the bottom petal only. Shade the top petal along each side.
- **Pink rose.** Lightly base-paint the rose petals with the salmon pink–Liquin mixture, keeping the centers light. On the large petal on the left, shade the right side a darker value. On the top petal, shade along the right side a darker value. Shade the remaining three petals along the top edge a darker value.
- **Pink rosebuds.** Lightly base-paint the rosebuds with the same mixture, keeping the centers light. Then shade the left sides a darker value.
- **Stems and calyxes of buds.** Base-paint the stems and calyxes of the buds with raw sienna; then shade the edges with chromium oxide green, keeping the centers light.
- **Rose leaves.** Base-paint the rose leaves with raw sienna, then shade with chromium oxide green. Place a curve on a leaf and shade with Prussian blue. Remove the curve, and paint some of the same color on the outer edge of the leaf. Repeat for each rose leaf.
- **Leaf of yellow flower on right.** Base-paint with raw sienna, then shade with chromium oxide green. Allow some of the raw sienna to show along the edges of the leaves.
- **Forget-me-nots.** Paint the edges of the petals with the blue mix for the forget-me-nots. Darken areas that are behind another petal.

- **Lilac leaf edge.** Paint the the leaf with raw sienna. Shade the right side with chromium oxide green, fading to the raw sienna. Then overshade the green with some Prussian blue.
- **Vase.** Paint all of the vase pieces with the pale yellow-white mixture. Then use the blue vase mixture to paint along the edges of each opening on the foot of the vase. On the horizontal vase piece, shade with the blue mixture along the sides and lower edge. Starting on the left side of the fluted top of the vase and working toward the center, shade just the left side of the flutes. Now move to the right side of the vase, and shade the flutes only on the right side.

**STENCIL NUMBER 3**

- **Lilac.** Paint each of the lilac petals with the lilac blue color. Then shade one edge of the petals a darker value, keeping the centers light.
- **Blue flowers.** Base-paint the petals of the blue flowers with the lilac blue color. Paint the flowers on the left a deeper value of the lilac color than the ones on the right.

  Using the round side of a curve, paint a fold in the petals of the flowers on the right.
- **White roses.** On the large rose, shade the lower edges of the top petal on the right with the Payne's gray–Liquin mixture. Shade along the top edge and left side of the lower right petal. On the left petal, shade along the right side, then shade a very fine edge along the left side. On the smaller white rose, shade the left petal on all sides. On the left petal, shade a fold in the petal starting at the dip in the petal on the left side and fade out quickly.
- **Forget-me-nots.** Paint the edges of the petals with the blue mixture for the forget-me-nots.
- **Carnation.** Lightly base-paint the petals of the carnation with the salmon pink color. Then shade along the lower edges of the top left, middle, and the top right petals. On the lower right petal, shade along the left side.
- **Yellow double daffodil.** Lightly base-paint the petals with the yellow flower mixture. On each of the petals, shade the edges that face the center of the flower with transparent gold ochre. Use the round side of a curve on each petal to create the fold, and shade with the same color.

**Stencil Number 4**

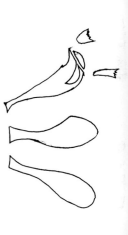

- **Red rose**. Base-paint the rose petals with alizarin crimson, keeping the centers light. On the top two petals, shade the lower edges darker. With a medium brush, shade the large lower petal along the bottom and up into the center of the petal, creating a ripple.
- **White dianthus**. On the left petal, paint the lower edges of the dianthus petals with the Payne's gray–Liquin mixture. Fade out quickly. On the right petal, shade the left side and along the outer edge of the petal.
- **Yellow flowers on right**. Lightly base-paint the petals of these two flowers with the yellow flower mixture, keeping the centers light. On the top flower, shade the petal along the upper and lower edges with transparent gold ochre.
- **Pink rose**. Lightly base-paint the rose petals with the salmon pink–Liquin mixture. Shade along the upper edge of the top left petal, the right side of the top right petal, and the upper edges of the other two petals.
- **Vase**. Paint the centers of the vase pieces with the pale yellow mixture. With the blue vase color, shade the fingerlike pieces along the edges, keeping the lower edge darker. Starting on the upper left side of the vase, shade the two flutes along the left side, the center flute along all edges, and the right flute piece on the right.
- **Rose leaves**. Base-paint the leaves with raw sienna, then shade the left side with chromium oxide green, fading to the raw sienna on the right. Place a curve on a leaf, and shade with Prussian blue. Remove the curve, and paint some Prussian blue on the left outer edge. Repeat for each rose leaf.
- **Pink rosebud calyxes and stems**. Base-paint the calyxes of the buds and stems with raw sienna, then shade the edges with chromium oxide green, keeping the centers light.
- **Lilac leaves**. Paint the leaves with raw sienna. On the left leaf, shade the left side with chromium oxide green, fading quickly. On the right leaf, shade the right side with the green, fading quickly.
- **Carnation leaves**. Base-paint the leaves lightly with chromium oxide green, then shade with some Prussian blue.

**STENCIL NUMBER 4**

- **Carnation**. Lightly base-paint the petals of the carnation with the salmon pink color. Shade along the lower edge and right side of the top left petal, the lower edge of the top middle petal, and the lower edge and top saw-toothed edge of the right petal.
- **Rose leaves**. Base-paint the leaves with raw sienna, then shade with chromium oxide green. Place a curve on a leaf, and shade with Prussian blue. Remove the curve, and paint some Prussian blue on the outer edge. Repeat for each rose leaf.
- **Calyxes of rosebuds and stems**. Base-paint the calyxes of the buds and stems with raw sienna, then shade the edges with chromium oxide green, keeping the centers light.
- **Lower yellow flower on right**. Base-paint the flower petal with the yellow flower color, keeping the center light. Shade the top edge with transparent gold ochre.
- **Calyx of yellow flower**. Base-paint the calyx with yellow ochre, then shade with chromium oxide green.
- **Pink rose**. Lightly base-paint the rose petals with the salmon pink–Liquin mixture, keeping the centers light. Shade the left side of the lower edge of the top right petal. On the top right petal, shade the outer edge, then the lower edge, creating a curve in the petal. On the other two petals, shade along the upper edges.
- **Red rose**. Base-paint the rose petals with alizarin crimson, keeping the centers light. Shade the lower edge of the left petal, the left side and lower edge of the top center petal, and the top and left side of the right petal.
- **White roses**. Lightly paint the petals with the Payne's gray–Liquin mixture. On the top petal of the large rose, use a small brush to shade some ripples from the top to the middle with the same mixture. On the lower petal, shade the upper edge. On the smaller rose, shade the petal along the lower edge. Then shade along the upper edge.
- **Yellow double daffodil**. Lightly base-paint the petals with the yellow flower mixture, then shade the edges that face the center with transparent gold ochre. Use the round side of a curve on the petals to create the fold, and shade with the same color.

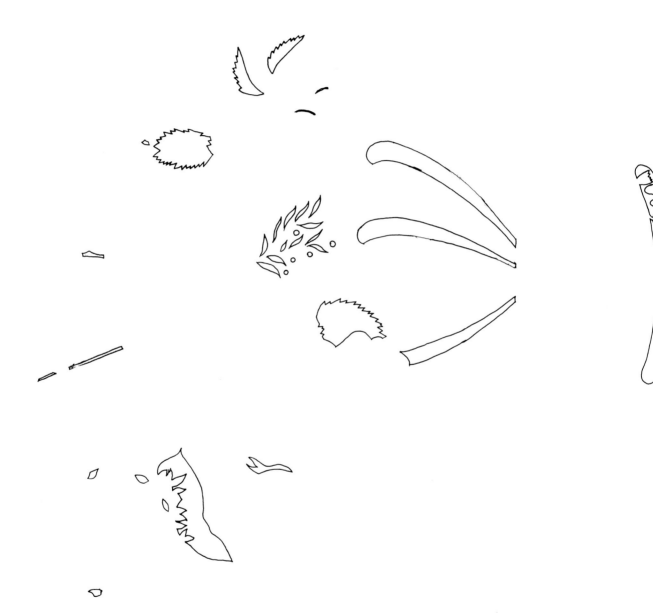

- **Forget-me-nots**. Paint the edges of the petals with the blue mixture for the forget-me-nots. Deepen any areas that are behind another petal.
- **Lilac**. Paint each of the lilac petals with the lilac blue color, then shade one edge a darker value, keeping the centers light.
- **Blue flowers**. Base-paint the petals of the blue flowers with the lilac blue color. On the right flowers, place the curve into position and shade along the curve.
- **Carnation leaves**. Base-paint the leaves with chromium oxide green, then shade with Prussian blue.
- **Vase**. Paint the centers of the vase pieces with pale yellow–white mixture, then paint along the edges with the blue vase mixture.
- **Lily of the valley**. Paint the outer edge of the lily of the valley with the Payne's gray–Liquin mixture.

## STENCIL NUMBER 5
- **Red rose**. Base-paint the rose petals with alizarin crimson, keeping the centers light. On the large petal, shade a deeper value along the top and lower edges. On the top petal, deepen the right and lower edges.
- **Yellow double daffodil**. Lightly base-paint the petal with the yellow flower color, then shade the top edge and upper left side with transparent gold ochre. Use the round side of a curve on the petal to create the fold, and shade with the same color.
- **Vase**. Paint the center of the vase piece with the pale yellow–white mixture. Then paint along the top and right side with the blue vase mixture, fading to the pale yellow near the center.
- **Lily of the valley leaves and stem**. Base-paint the leaves and stem with yellow ochre, then shade with chromium oxide green.
- **Rose leaves**. Base-paint the leaves with raw sienna, then shade the edges with chromium oxide green. Place a curve on a leaf, and shade with Prussian blue. Remove the curve, and paint some Prussian blue on the outer edge. Repeat for each rose leaf.

- **Rosebud calyxes and stems**. Base-paint the bud calyxes and stems with raw sienna, then shade the edges with chromium oxide green, keeping the centers light.
- **Lilac**. Paint each of the lilac petals with the lilac blue color, then shade one edge a darker value, keeping the centers light.
- **Forget-me-nots**. Paint the edges of the petals with the blue mixture for the forget-me-nots. Deepen any areas that are behind another petal.
- **Carnation leaf**. Base-paint the leaf with chromium oxide green, then shade with Prussian blue. Paint the upper edge a slightly darker value.

## STENCIL NUMBER 6
- **Lilac**. Paint each of the lilac petals with the lilac blue color, then shade one edge a darker value, keeping the center light.
- **Center spray of blue buds and leaves**. Paint these buds with some Prussian blue mixed with Liquin to make a pale blue. Paint the leaves with chromium oxide green.
- **Lilac leaf**. Base-paint the leaf with raw umber, then shade very lightly with chromium oxide green. Shade the lower part of the leaf with some Prussian blue.
- **Stems, rose leaves, and calyx**. Base-paint the leaves with raw sienna, then shade the edges with chromium oxide green. Place a curve on a leaf and shade with Prussian blue. Remove the curve and paint some Prussian blue on the outer edge of the leaf. Repeat with curve and Prussian blue with each rose leaf. Base-paint the stems with yellow ochre, then shade with chromium oxide green.
- **Vase**. Starting on the left side of the fluted top of the vase and working to the center, shade just the left side of the flute with the blue vase mixture. Now move to the right side of the fluted top and shade only on the right side of the flutes. On the foot of the vase, shade the upper and lower edges of the base.

DETAIL
- **Stamens in dianthus and daffodil**. Mix some Turpenoid and raw sienna. With the liner brush, paint some dots in the center of the daffodil randomly and beside the dianthus center on the petals. Mix Turpenoid with some chromium oxide green and Prussian blue, and paint some green-blue dots among the yellow ones.
- **Carnation**. Mix some Turpenoid with the salmon pink, and add some alizarin crimson golden. Add more Turpenoid if necessary. Paint some fine lines on each of the carnation petals. These lines should start at the base of each petal and fade out past the middle.

- **Stems, thorns, veins, and baby's breath stems**. Mix some Turpenoid with a blend of chromium oxide green and Prussian blue, and add a drop of Skin So Soft oil. Paint the veins in the leaves. Between the blue flowers on the left and the red rose, paint a bunch of branches for the baby's breath. On the lily of the valley, paint a stem connecting the flowers and the leaves. Paint tiny little thorns on all the rose stems and calyxes, plus some wispy lines at the end of each calyx. Add some stems here and there in between the lilac flowers.
- **Baby's breath**. Using the salmon color, paint little dots around the stems of the baby's breath.

# Framing

*Lilies by Linda E. Brubaker.* COLLECTION OF MR. AND MRS. JAMES BRUBAKER

A frame can either enhance or detract from the beauty of a work of art, so there are a few things you need to consider when choosing a frame for your theorem. Is your painting meant to be a formal piece or folk art? Will it be hung in a casual or traditional setting? Is it large or small? Does the frame look aesthetically pleasing with the particular painting? Following are some examples of different frame choices.

These two baby theorems are similar, but each frame gives the painting it holds a different feel. The red grained frame is slightly wider than the gold frame, but it does not overpower the picture. If the grained frame were even a few inches wider, however, it would dominate the painting and detract from it. This frame is well suited for a country-style home, whereas the gold frame looks more formal and also has a softer appearance. The brown line in the gold frame complements the brown corn shocks, whereas the red grained frame picks up the red in the rabbit's jacket and the flag. In both cases, the frames complement the artwork.

*Commemorative Birth Announcement by Linda E. Brubaker.* COLLECTION OF MR. AND MRS. LEE LERNER

*Commemorative Birth Announcement by Linda E. Brubaker.* COLLECTION OF MR. AND MRS. STEVEN BRUBAKER

*Compote of Fruit by Robert Flachbarth.* COLLECTION OF ARTIST

Several versions of this composition, painted in different mediums, are on display in the Abby Aldrich Rockefeller Museum in Williamsburg, Virginia. The same design was used in these two velvet theorems by Robert Flachbarth, but they were painted and framed differently. The first was painted as closely as possible to the original design, owned by the Historic Society of Early American Decoration. For this theorem, the artist chose a gold frame that enhances the rich golden color in the base of the compote and the peach and pear. The second version is mounted in a burled wood frame that has hints of brushed gold on the molded edge. This frame reflects the rich reds and warm browns of the branches. Each of these paintings has its beauty heightened by the frame choice.

For this Basket of Flowers theorem, painted by Ann Kline, the artist chose a beautiful antique mahogany frame. The deep red of the rose in the center picks up some of the red nuances in the mahogany, and the swirls in the wood echo the flow of the petals in the carnation. Notice how the piece is slightly lower in the frame, giving it a well-balanced look. This proved to be a very good use of an old frame, giving it a new life while wonderfully enhancing the theorem.

*Flower Basket by Ann Kline.* COLLECTION OF ARTIST

A gold frame sets off this Basket of Flowers theorem that I painted. This frame works for several reasons. The roping on the outer edge echoes the rope design on the handle and the foot of the basket, while the round beaded inner edge reflects the round centers of the flowers. The gold tones in the frame pick up the various gold shades in the flowers and the brown stripe complements the browns in the basket. Both frames work well with the Basket of Flower paintings.

*Flower Basket by Linda E. Brubaker.* COLLECTION OF MR. AND MRS. JAMES BRUBAKER

Two versions of Apples on a Marble Slab were rendered from the same design of an antique theorem painted in watercolors on paper. The first one is an exact copy of the original, but painted in oils on velvet. The colors are very soft, and the frame reflects the painting's delicate appearance. It also enhances the coloring in the three apples, and the faint gray-blue line in the frame mirrors the blue in the morning glories and the marble base.

*Apples on a Marble Slab by Linda E. Brubaker.* COLLECTION OF MR. AND MRS. JAMES BRUBAKER

Even though the design is the same, this second painting is very different. Here the artist's bold use of color in the theorem requires a bolder frame. In this blue-grained frame, the depth of color matches the depth in the blue grapes. Notice also how the undulating grain painted on the frame mirrors the movement in the tendrils of the morning glories and the flow of the veins in the leaves. Thus again, both frame choices complement the paintings.

When looking for a frame for your lovely theorem, keep in mind nuances such as those described in the comparisons above, and choose a frame that will complement and enhance your work.

*Apples on a Marble Slab by Linda E. Brubaker.* COLLECTION OF MR. AND MRS. JAMES BRUBAKER

# Gallery

A rtists in the nineteenth century began embellishing theorems with gold, beads, crystals, mother-of-pearl, mica, and bronzing powders. These items were used individually or in combination to add texture and depth. The vivid colors of the theorems are enhanced by the intricate embellishments, which create a striking effect. Bronzing powder and gold also lend warmth and richness to the piece.

Contemporary theorem artists, some of whom are my students, painted the following works.

Above: *Oriental Pheasants in a Basket of Flowers by Linda E. Brubaker. Inspired by the Gilded Age, this theorem is embellished with 18- and 23-karat gold leaf, Austrian crystals, glass beads, and a metallic ribbon.* COLLECTION OF AUTHOR

*Summer Flowers
in a Basket
by Jean Bellis.*
COLLECTION OF ARTIST

*Basket of Flowers
by Olivia Hill.*
PRIVATE COLLECTION

*Roses in a Summer Garden by Joan Bradford.* COLLECTION OF ARTIST

*Basket of Fruit on a Blue Table by Alexandra Perrot.* COLLECTION OF ARTIST

*Oriental Bowl of Fruit by Ann Kline.*

COLLECTION OF ARTIST

*Goldfinches by Donna Smith.*
COLLECTION OF MR. AND MRS. JAMES BRUBAKER

*Butterflies by Linda E. Brubaker.*
*These butterflies were enhanced with*
*metallic powders and Austrian crystals.*
COLLECTION OF AUTHOR

*Bird and Geraniums with*
*reverse glass mat in grained*
*frame by Linda E. Brubaker.*
COLLECTION OF MR. AND MRS. RICHARD SENFT

*Rainbow Trout by Linda E. Brubaker.*
COLLECTION OF MR. AND MRS. STEVEN BRUBAKER

*Golden Bird by Linda E. Brubaker.*
COLLECTION OF MR. AND MRS. RICHARD SENFT

*Ringneck in Flight by Linda E. Brubaker.*
COLLECTION OF MR. AND MRS. STEVEN BRUBAKER

*Merry Christmas by Linda E. Brubaker. Inspired by a nineteenth-century postcard, this scene is embellished with opalescent glitter and gold and silver paint.*
COLLECTION OF MR. AND MRS. SCOTT GEIGER

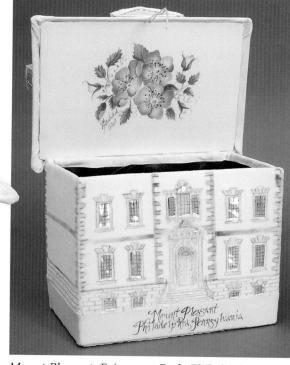

*Mount Pleasant, Fairmount Park, Philadelphia, Pennsylvania, by Linda E. Brubaker, 2001. The silk, velvet, and paper theorem covering this hand-sewn box is enhanced with mother-of-pearl, opalescent glitter, and paint. The roof opens to revel a silk painting of roses.* COLLECTION OF AUTHOR

# SUPPLIES AND RESOURCES

**A. C. Moore**
www.acmoore.com

**The Art Store**
29 E. King St.
Lancaster, PA 17602
717-394-4600

**Art Supply Warehouse (ASW)**
800-995-6778
www.aswexpress.com

**The Artist's Club**
800-845-6507
www.artistsclub.com

**Dick Blick Art Materials**
800-447-8192
www.dickblick.com

**Historical Society of Early American Decoration (HSEAD)**
P.O. Box 30
Cooperstown, NY 13326
607-547-5667
http://hsead.org
info@hsead.org
Historical theorem patterns

**Jerry's Artarama**
*The Jerry's Catalog*
800-827-8478
www.jerrysartarama.com

**Jo-Ann Fabric and Craft Stores**
www.joann.com
Velvet

**Michaels**
www.michaels.com

**P.J.'s Decorative Stencils**
21 Carter St.
Newburyport, MA 01950
518-330-5555
www.PJstencils.com
PJ@PJstencils.com
Stencil film

**Scharff Brushes, Inc.**
P.O. Box 745
165 Commerce Dr.
Fayetteville, GA 30214
800-724-2733
www.artbrush.com
Scharff@artbrush.com
Brushes

**Welch Haven**
622 Coleman Lane
Galax, VA 24333
276-236-6626
Velvet

*Adaptation of* Man with English Guitar and Sheep *by Linda E. Brubaker, 1998. Adapted from a watercolor painting on paper by an unknown artist, this idyllic Gothic romance scene leads us into the outdoors and encourages us to day-dream. The original is in the collection of the Smithsonian Institution.* COLLECTION OF JAMES AND LINDA BRUBAKER

*Wedding Theorem by Linda E. Brubaker.* COLLECTION OF MR. AND MRS. STEVEN BRUBAKER

# BIBLIOGRAPHY

Bernet, Frances. "Theorems, Old and New." *The Decorator* (Historical Society of Early American Decoration) 46, no. 1. (Fall/Winter 1991–92): 24–30.

Hampton, Madeline W. "Velvet Paintings (Trompe l'Oeil)." *The Decorator* (Historical Society of Early American Decoration) 20, no. 1. (Fall 1965): 8–10.

Herr, Patricia T. *The Ornamental Branches*. Virginia Beach: Donning Company, 1996.

Karr, Louise. "Paintings on Velvet." *Antiques*. (September 1931): 162–65.

Lefko, Linda Carter and Barbara Knickerbocker. *The Art of Theorem Painting*. New York: Viking Studio Books, 1994.

Lipman, Jean. *American Primitive Painting*. New York: Dover Publications, 1972.

McIntyre, Vickie. "Theorem Paintings." *Early American Life*. Volume XII. (August 1981): 28–29, 62–65.

Polley, Robert L., ed. *America's Folk Art*. Waukesha, WI: Country Beautiful, 1971.

Rumford, Beatrix T. *American Folk Paintings from the Abby Aldrich Folk Art Center*. Boston: Little, Brown and Company, 1988.

Smith, Linda Joan. "Parlor Paintings." *Country Home*. (October 1990): 108–14, 148–49.

Stein, Aaron Mare. "The Still-Life in American 'Primitive' Art." *The Fine Arts*. Volume 19 (June 1932): 14–16, 42–43.

Underhill, Emilie. "Velvet Painting." *The Decorator*. (Historical Society of Early American Decoration) 43, no. 1 (Fall 1963): 3–9.

*Summer Fruit by Linda E. Brubaker. The artist adapted a Currier and Ives print titled* Fruit of the Seasons *for this theorem painting on velvet.* COLLECTION OF JAMES AND LINDA E. BRUBAKER

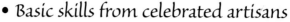